Praise for Growing Confident Leaders

"*Growing Confident Leaders* offers guiding ideas and concepts that can help leaders figure out their best path forward. The book distinguishes leadership from management and acknowledges that both are necessary. It elegantly describes AJ's Heart of the Matter leadership model and makes the essential point that everybody needs a sense of meaning, hope, and trust in the work they do. The book provides many leadership examples and illustrations and serves as a useful guide for anyone aspiring to lead others."

—**BJORN BILLHARDT**, CEO of Abilitie
and coauthor of *The 12-Week MBA*

"In *Growing Confident Leaders*, AJ Josefowitz provides a framework that allows people to go from being managers to being leaders. Packed with wisdom from decades of experience with executives around the country, Josefowitz provides readers with a chance to explore the key skills needed to transform organizations, along with insightful questions to spur reflection about their own leadership journey."

—**ART MARKMAN**, founding director of the
Human Dimensions of Organizations program
at the University of Texas at Austin
and author of *Bring Your Brain to Work*

"There are so many books out there about leadership. What makes this book different is it offers strong conceptual roots. After reading this book, you will think more deeply about leadership. AJ Josefowitz offers readers a model of what leaders need to do to succeed—one of the most insightful models I have encountered after teaching leadership for decades. *Growing Confident Leaders* is filled with intriguing tales from the author's personal experience coaching major corporate leaders from around the world. His lessons learned from over forty years of coaching very successful leaders are summarized in memorable and impactful ways. Plus, the book includes seminar-like questions that will get every reader reflecting on what they can do to bolster their effectiveness as a leader. You will become a better leader, and perhaps a better person, by reading this book."

—**JOHN A. DALY,** Liddell Professor of Communication and TCB Professor of Management at the University of Texas at Austin and author of *Advocacy: Championing Ideas and Influencing Others*

GROWING CONFIDENT LEADERS

A POWERFUL MODEL FOR DEVELOPING SKILLS TO MOTIVATE AND INSPIRE

AJ JOSEFOWITZ

RIVER GROVE BOOKS

Published by River Grove Books
Austin, TX
www.rivergrovebooks.com

Distributed by River Grove Books

Design and composition by Greenleaf Book Group
Cover design by Greenleaf Book Group
Cover images used under license from
©Shutterstock.com/Victoria Sergeeva;
©Shutterstock.com/Nikolaeva

Publisher's Cataloging-in-Publication data is available.

Print ISBN: 978-1-63299-756-2

eBook ISBN: 978-1-63299-757-9

First Edition

To my inspirations: Emily, Allison, and Alexander.

And to the next generation: Benjamin and Jacob.

Contents

Introduction

Henry Miller once wrote, "No one is great enough or wise enough to surrender our destiny to. The only way in which anyone can lead us is to restore to us the belief in our own thinking." To me, that sentiment rings true. At its core, it reflects a bias for self-initiation and confidence about the work to be done. Henry Miller's message is to never give ourselves over to others to lead us. Effective leaders already understand this and know that the best way to lead is to help those they lead—their constituents—feel confidence in themselves.

It's not a complex notion; in fact, it's quite simple. And it's the simple ideas that often lead us to important insights that help challenge and shape us by expanding our choices and directions. In fact, each one of us is always leading in one way or another. Like Russian dolls, one embedded in the next, so too is each one of us embedded—and leading—in different roles: at work, home, school, in our organizations, communities, and sports teams. And of course, there's always self-leadership.

Inside an organization, however, the management hierarchy can overwhelm—or supplant—leadership. We look to people at the top of the hierarchy to provide leadership. This makes sense, provided the best leaders keep getting promoted to the top of the hierarchy. Yet we also know that people without direct reports, those who aren't in traditional management roles, nonetheless lead through influence and persuasion. Maybe it's not a leadership responsibility but, rather, a leadership capability. Leadership is everywhere, and at its simplest, it's self-leadership, deciding whether to get out of bed each morning or to roll over and go back to sleep.

From the late 1980s to the mid-1990s, I was responsible for executive development at a US Midwest-based global Fortune 500 company. Around that time, two local entrepreneurs launched a speaker series, The Masters Forum, with the tagline, "tomorrow's ideas today." They did an exceptional job of identifying and securing vanguard thought leaders to address their forum. For example, they brought Stephen Covey to town before his *Seven Habits* book had even been published.

I attended most of those sessions and met many of the speakers. The entire experience—the lectures, the readings, and the conversations—was always interesting and helpful. I shared some of those ideas with my clients. In some instances, I used ideas I'd gathered from the forum to design and implement organizational development initiatives to help improve leadership and team effectiveness in my client organizations. I really enjoyed that work.

Of the many leadership thinkers I was exposed to during those years, a few stood out because they still stand out; in other words, their ideas and perspectives about leadership and organization dynamics in the 1990s and earlier remain as relevant today. Two speakers in particular influenced me greatly. Warren Bennis, who passed away in 2014, most captured my attention and imagination with his notion that leadership is an art, not a science, and that like art, much of what matters is best *experienced*, and trying to explain it is always inadequate.

Another great leadership scholar whose work interested me and whose personal story I admired greatly was John Gardner. Among other roles, Gardner was President Lyndon B. Johnson's Secretary of Health, Education, and Welfare. He also founded Common Cause and wrote extensively about leadership. His positive impact on the understanding of leadership was enormous. In 1982, after a lifelong career in Washington, DC, Gardner relocated to Stanford University, where he became a faculty member till he passed in 2002. In particular, I always admired Gardner's ability to reinvent himself later in life when he moved from politics to academia, and from the East Coast (Washington, DC) to the West Coast (Stanford University), two distant and different environments. His book *On* Leadership helped me understand that leadership is a means to an end, not an end in itself.

Gardner helped me understand that leadership is but one ingredient in the pursuit of its most worthy end goal: to accomplish group purpose. A focus on the group and tying leadership to that helped me understand that the relationships between leaders and constituents are at the heart of leadership.

In 1995, I moved to Austin, Texas, for the opportunity to work for a leader I greatly admired. I thought this man was forward-thinking, highly ethical, and charismatic. To me, he was a great leader because he was a relational leader, someone whose effectiveness was drawn from the bonds he formed with the people around him.

One example of his relational leadership instinct was that he ate breakfast every Friday morning with people from the customer service organization. They always sat at the center table in the cafeteria, in full view of everyone. Anybody who walked into the cafeteria on a Friday morning would see the leader, Bill, holding court with a dozen or more customer service employees.

Bill was particularly astute at recognizing and engaging in leadership activities that yielded large dividends for his investments. The breakfast cost him 90 minutes a week. The return on that investment was the rapport with and admiration of many customer-facing employees who participated with him in that weekly practice (it bought him influence). I'm confident that Bill's Friday morning breakfasts with the customer service organization helped them deepen their sense of their work's importance. It's not too far-fetched to consider that even people who were not part of that group and only witnessed those gatherings from afar benefited from that exposure as well.

Bill appreciated the value of effective leadership and charged me to design and deliver a leadership workshop that would promote his leadership views and how he wanted the organization to grow. He left to become the CEO of another company about a year later, but not before I designed and delivered the inaugural sessions of the workshop he'd requested—and that he attended. That experience set me on a path to investigate and design leadership development experiences and processes that helped people improve their leadership effectiveness and emphasized the most important responsibility of leaders: to grow new leaders.

The Heart of the Matter

Over the decades of studying and teaching aspects of leadership, I developed a rubric I call the Heart of the Matter model (see Figure 0.1), and I used that model to organize this book. This model explains a particular perspective about leader–constituent interactions. The Heart of the Matter guides the growth and development of confident leaders.

By nature, culture, and education, I'm a reductionist. I like to look for the center, the core, the essence of something out of which other things grow. Similarly, I like to go as far upstream as possible to understand how things start—to get at their root causes. It seems to me that all stories of leadership begin with an aspiration to accomplish something important: a larger purpose.

The views about leadership expressed in this book are rooted in the idea that leadership is an art expressed and experienced through interactions—primarily interactions between leaders and their constituents. At its heart, leadership is an influence relationship between leaders and constituents. This relationship reflects mutual purposes, and those shared purposes give rise to collective motivations and opportunities to create new, improved, and important products, services, and processes.

The influence relationships between leaders and their constituents, who aim to accomplish important work, revolve around three core motivators: meaning, hope, and trust. In Figure 0.1, depicting the model, you'll find those core motivators in the center column, noted as values the constituents need.

THE HEART OF THE MATTER MODEL

Leaders help constituents find...		In service of their need for...		To help create...
Primary Dimensions:				
Purpose	⪢	Meaning	⪢	Goals & Objectives
Optimism	⪢	Hope	⪢	Energy & Creativity
Integrity	⪢	Trust	⪢	Reliability & Accountability
Supporting Dimension:				
Support	⪢	Growth	⪢	Self-Reliance & Leadership Development

Figure 0.1

These core motivators—meaning, hope, and trust—are elemental, fundamental, and foundational. They're elemental in that they cannot be reduced any further. These are the lowest relational common denominators between people. They are fundamental because they convey importance: They matter to the well-being of the people, individually and collectively, and have great influence. And they are also foundational in that they are bedrock, principled, set, and durable. They can be built upon.

Meaning, hope, and trust are essential features of interactions between people working together to get something important accomplished—and that's the art of leadership.

MEANING

Purpose is what a group is trying to accomplish, and *meaning* describes the personal attachments that individuals bring to that effort. These attachments vary from person to person, but everyone is motivated when they believe their work has meaning. In effective, artful relationships, leaders help their constituents discover the organization's purpose and connect that to their individual sense of meaning.

HOPE

Another core motivator is hope, a conviction that what needs to be achieved can be. Hope helps leaders and their constituents embrace drive and persistence. It helps them retain buoyancy, the ability to bounce back up when dragged down, and bolsters a sense of resilience. Without that, many if not most people would likely abandon their missions after some number of setbacks.

Years ago, prominent psychologist and scholar Martin Seligman observed that researchers in the field of psychology often studied what is wrong with human behavior and why, but they didn't investigate successes and achievements nearly as much. From that insight, Seligman created the discipline called positive psychology, the scientific study of strengths that enable individuals and communities to thrive. It helps explain hope as a core performance motivator.[1]

TRUST

Trust is the third core motivator and the one that ties the first two together. Trust demands the most attention and maintenance and is the motivator that shapes how people behave with each other. It connects leaders and constituents and influences constituent relationships with others. Very little, if anything, gets accomplished alone, and nothing helps people work together more than trusting interactions. The degree of trust that people share sets the limits for collective effectiveness. Trust is at the heart of human emotions and relationships.

Motivational Pairs

Effective leaders help constituents discover purpose, optimism, and integrity in response to what their constituents need and want—meaning, hope, and trust. Those motivational pairs circumscribe important interaction dynamics between leaders and

1 Martin Seligman, "Figuring Out Happiness," *Princeton Alumni Weekly*, October 8, 2008.

their constituents. Constituents are motivated by meaningful work, and effective leaders help them discover work purpose. Similarly, work is always better (more productive and with the right amount of stress) when it is infused with a sense of hope, when there is a plan and confidence that it can be achieved. Effective leaders convey confidence and optimism in ways that help their constituents become more hopeful, energized, and committed to the challenges of their work. Finally, effective leaders model integrity in ways that help people trust them and become more trusting and trustworthy themselves.

The model is an organizer. It provides a road map for leader–constituent interaction that takes shape in specific circumstances and situations by specific leaders and constituents. Purpose and meaning, optimism and hope, and integrity and trust intertwine and work together to create a group's performance and effectiveness.

Having leaders and constituents share mutual purposes is critical to the foundation of all leadership work. Effective leaders work hard to understand common issues and how best to forge common understanding and agreement. Effective leaders don't coerce or bully their constituents. Effective leaders understand that influence works best when it flows both ways: Leaders need to influence their constituents, and constituents need to feel heard by their leaders as well.

These core motivators are essential for leading a purposeful life. For work to contribute to that, it needs to offer opportunities to do important things and confidence that working with others can achieve desired outcomes. Trust is what helps people work effectively with other people.

Meaning, hope, and trust are what help us get out of bed in the morning. In the absence of these core motivators, we might just roll over and go back to sleep. Artful, effective leaders help people discover their purpose and attach meaning to it. They help energize people with convictions that goals can be accomplished. They also model credibility and integrity that build, facilitate, and influence trusting relationships.

We all know that trust is critical for collaborative work and that it is very hard to build and very easy to destroy. Effective leaders build trustworthiness by consistently modeling credibility and integrity.

Warren Bennis, whose work has influenced much of my thinking about leadership, had a distinguished academic career both as a university president and professor and was a widely recognized scholar and author about leadership. I once heard him tell a story about how he got interested in studying leadership. He grew up with older brothers who were identical twins. He said they were so identical that, at times, he wasn't 100% sure which one he was with. He described that one brother was very outgoing and easily able to engage with and influence people, while the other twin was much quieter, a smart and good person but not someone who comfortably engaged with others. That experience with twin brothers initiated his curiosity about leadership. I always liked that story.

I've been working with the Heart of the Matter model for more than 20 years, and although the work always adapts to change, the model has remained remarkably stable. The Heart of the Matter continues to offer helpful suggestions about how to think about leadership and how to lead.

This book shares those ideas through the lens of that three-column depiction. The book can be a how-to guide. The book is sprinkled with reflective questions about your leadership practices. I hope you take the time to consider some. Most important, I hope reading this book provokes your thinking about leadership, how you approach leading, and especially how to become a better leader.

What I most hope you get from this book is an enhanced way of thinking about leadership, one that feels organic and is easy to remember as you embrace the elemental, fundamental, and foundational aspects of the model's core values.

The topic of leadership is broad. Circumstances may require one path, while personalities direct a different one. What works today might not work tomorrow, and what works for one group might fail with another.

It's impossible to write a one-size-fits-all prescription for effective leadership, and that's because leadership is art. It is also an approach. The Heart of the Matter model doesn't offer prescriptions for right or wrong as much as an orientation to leadership, a way of thinking about leadership that helps guide how best to lead.

I want this book to be a catalyst for helping readers become increasingly effective at instigating positive and purposeful change. My hope is to mirror Henry Miller's notion that it's better to build confidence from within than to blindly let someone else lead us. The core of leadership comes from within.

Leadership gets executed through confidence. Absent confidence, we'll have ideas at best, but they will likely be left on the drawing board. There's no single way to build confidence and there's no simple solution. Confidence has its roots in success, the belief and conviction of succeeding. Effective leaders understand what gives their constituents belief and hope for success and use every opportunity to convey such teachable moments.

CHAPTER 1

The Foundations of Leadership

Leadership is a means to an end. Accomplishing group purpose is the ultimate objective that effective leadership helps accomplish. Yet leadership is just one of many ingredients that help a person or an organization accomplish something of benefit for themselves and others. In addition to leadership, accomplishing a group's purpose also requires resources, strategies, structure, rules, policies, protocols, and other elements.

People often say leadership is the most important ingredient for accomplishing a group's purpose. I say it may not be more important, but it's certainly as important as any other.

Without leadership, an entity drifts and ultimately loses control—often to unhelpful influences.

A Context for Leadership

Any time there's a group of people trying to accomplish something, there's a need for leadership. A leader's pressing first questions are "Who is my group?" and "What is our common purpose?" These are the grounding truths that anchor leadership's reason for being. Leading has greater impact and becomes more efficient as leaders grow and as they deepen their understanding and appreciation for the answers to these questions.

Reflection

- Who is your group?
- What is your group's purpose?

Viewing leadership as an enabler helps bring into sharper focus the contributions that effective leadership can enable. It helps make those contributions—real or aspirational—more tangible to appreciate, influence, and develop. But the unique challenges of leadership can be difficult; effective leaders are always searching for helpful tools and fresh perspectives that can help them become stronger leaders.

Leadership and Management

A helpful way to begin an examination of leadership is to contrast it with management. Virtually all organizations have a common purpose: to thrive and grow. Organizations want to live and grow for the benefit of their stakeholders. Leaders, the people responsible for accomplishing that goal, use different orientations and skill sets to make that happen: management and leadership.

Management is about driving predictability, and leadership is about driving change. Leadership and management sometimes engage separate processes that require different skill sets to help organizations, teams, and individuals—including oneself—to make progress. Management and leadership are like salt and pepper: They are both necessary, and neither one alone is sufficient. Neither is better or more important than the other. The key is for them to coexist in proper balance.

Balance is a recurring and important theme in the Heart of the Matter.

Reflection

- What does balance look like for you and your organization?
- Where are you now?
- What would help you achieve better balance?

Furthermore, management is about the here and now, whereas leadership is about the future. The trick is discovering and focusing on the appropriate balance between the two—the so-called Goldilocks state, when things are not too hot, not too cold, but just right.

Effective leaders are always balancing their measures of execution (management) and strategy (leadership). The most effective leaders understand the distinction between the two, the different outcomes they enable, and the balance needed between them.

Table 1.1 shows the differences between managers and leaders. As you read it, consider your own leadership style and assess which way you veer and with what balance.

MANAGER VS. LEADER	
The Manager	**The Leader**
• administers	• innovates
• is a copy	• is an original
• maintains	• develops
• focuses on systems and structure	• focuses on people
• relies on control	• inspires trust
• has a short-range view	• has a long-range perspective
• asks how and when	• asks what and why
• eyes the bottom line	• eyes the horizon
• imitates	• originates

• accepts the status quo	• challenges the status quo
• is the classic good soldier	• is their own person
• does things right	• does the right thing

Table 1.1

Effective leaders are mindful of the amount of time and effort they spend on each style. They understand that too much management and too little leadership can create bureaucracy, whereas too much leadership without enough management can create chaos.

Discovering the balance between predictability and change is one of the core challenges of effective leadership. Too much predictability can cause organizations to lose their capacity to identify needed change, whereas too much change can create consequences of instability, uncertainty, and confusion. Effective leaders lead change that moves toward balance.

Three Vital Tools

Three important tools that effective leaders use to appropriately balance their focus on leadership and management are these: alignment with others, prioritization, and delegation.

ALIGNMENT

Aligning with others—be they team members, other organizations, customers, clients, suppliers, and even governments—can provide leaders with perspectives that help shape their sense of what's needed to achieve balance. The more alignment the better. Effective leaders want their views of reality to connect with the views of others with whom they share common objectives.

PRIORITIZATION

Creating priorities creates balance, too. There is always more to do than the time available to get things done, and learning to prioritize helps leaders understand that the key to juggling is knowing which balls are made of glass and which are made of rubber.

DELEGATION

Finally, the art of delegating and understanding which leadership responsibilities can be handled effectively by others and which cannot be helps leaders along their perpetual journey in search of balance. The dynamics of alignment, prioritization, and delegation can all contribute to more balanced approaches to leadership.

BALANCE

The question of leadership always comes down to a question of balance. When is more leadership needed? When is more management needed? How should time be distributed between leading and managing?

In my experience as a coach and consultant, I've seen more leaders default to management because it tends to yield tangible results compared to leadership's focus on the future, which is inherently more uncertain.

Balance: The Horizontal Teeter-Totter

The Goldilocks moment, when an entity is in balance—not too hot, not too cold, but just right—is what effective leaders search for to guide their organizations forward. Picture a teeter-totter in balance; the weights on both sides are distanced from the fulcrum so that the teeter-totter at rest is perfectly horizontal. It's balanced.

The real world is much more dynamic and fluid. In the real world, things are shifting all the time, and only rarely is the fulcrum set or stable for long. The real-world leadership challenge is recognizing, influencing, and setting the fulcrum to help bring balance to the entire organization. Balance, the Goldilocks moment, is what all effective leaders and constituents are trying to achieve, although that's often difficult because of the constant forces pushing for change.

An organization or an individual is in balance when the right amount of predictability and change are present—and also in balance—in the work being done. Effective leaders understand the dynamics of change and predictability, and they pay attention.

How do you know if or when you're out of balance? Arguably we're always out of balance. Balance is something that we're always striving for but never quite attain. In the world of Six Sigma, the term *entitlement* means the idealized, preferred future state that can never be reached. Entitlement is always on the horizon. Entitlement is something to strive for. Similarly, so is balance. Effective leaders are always striving to guide themselves and their organizations toward better, more sustainable balance. The effective leader is always moving in the direction of better balance.

In my experience, the personification of one such leader who knew how to seek out balance was that executive I mentioned earlier. This man ran a $2 billion global business, which was organized into four divisions of similar size. For nine months, I was responsible for his organization's leadership development.

During much of that time, I worked on a special project to build and deliver a leadership workshop for his organization's VPs through supervisors, meaning all those who managed other people. Working with this man gave me an up-close view of his ways of thinking and acting. My tenure with him was short but unforgettable, unfortunately, because nine months after I got there, he was recruited to be the CEO of another company.

From my view, he acted more in the role of leader but did so without compromising his management responsibilities. In that regard, he was balanced. I witnessed and experienced the outcomes of his efforts to build, sustain, and grow his business's supply chain organization. Each of his four divisions had its own supply chain manager. He orchestrated their synergy and overlap, and his division VPs managed their respective organization's supply chain matters.

He exploited opportunities to bring people together. He met with the four supply chain managers on a regular basis. The leadership workshop that he commissioned brought executives, managers, and supervisors together to share their common experiences. He was present for at least part of every session delivered, perhaps 20 in all. He was successful at developing a culture and environment that confronted challenges as opportunities, and this served to energize the constituents in every corner of his large organization.

His ability to keep the teeter-totter in balance—with management on one side and leadership on the other—taught me a lot about the art of leadership. Let's turn now from the importance of balance to look at the types of forces that upend that horizontal seesaw: the forces of change.

CHAPTER 2

Leadership and Change

Change is leadership's essential desired outcome. Leadership and change are inseparable. Discovering and maintaining the balance between predictability and change is what effective leaders are always doing, trading off one for the other.

Effective leaders understand the character of change and human behavior in general. They have experiences, developed values, and perspectives about human nature. The more experience and insight leaders have about the nature of change, the more effective they are at leading it.

Years ago, I had a client who radically altered his organization's interface with their clients. He segmented customers into three categories based on their growth potential and gave priority to customers in growing businesses. These so-called key accounts had a dedicated workforce that focused only on them. In some instances, key account managers were embedded in their customers' organizations, colocating with those customers to better understand their needs and to be there to service them more quickly and comprehensively. These key accounts were given a lot of time and attention; they were viewed as strategic partners. They could be very demanding but were generally considered to be worth the effort.

The second category of customers was judged to be essential, because they provided a steady stream of business, although their growth trajectory was not as steep. They provided a predictable and profitable revenue stream.

The third category of customers was not strategically critical, because they offered neither growth potential nor a consistent and steady stream of business. They were customers who had been around for quite a long time, and the organization members charged with serving them worked to move them into the first or second category as much as possible. If no progress was apparent, the organization expended much less time and energy on them and even stopped servicing some of them.

Reordering, regrouping, and reclassifying these customers helped the entire organization go to market more efficiently.

Thinking versus Acting

Is it easier to think your way into a new way of acting or to act your way into a new way of thinking? Of course, the answer is that they're both necessary in balance.

Research conducted on how pediatric cardiologists performed diagnoses found that novices tended to collect a lot of data before generating hypotheses. That's "thinking your way into a new way of acting." In contrast, experts started generating hypotheses as soon as they collected their first bit of data and discarded hypotheses that were not supported by subsequently collected data.[2] That's "acting your way into a new way of thinking."

It seems that acting one's way into a new way of thinking is more prone to getting things started and moving, so it helps to have guardrails. The other direction can lead to analysis paralysis, so checks are needed there as well. Of course, it's always best to be appropriately balanced.

Reflection

- How do you analyze situations that create challenges and need to be addressed?
- Do you value the advice of counsel as much as, less than, or more than the value of reports and data?
- How often are your decisions driven by gut feelings?
- Where are you on the analysis paralysis to just-do-it scale of action and activity?

---

2 P. Hobus et al., "Contextual Factors in the Activation of First Diagnostic Hypotheses," *Medical Education* 21, no. 6 (November 1987), https://pubmed.ncbi.nlm.nih.gov/3696019/.

Making Change Happen

Aging is the only change that happens effortlessly. All other changes require work, whether that be resistance to or support for the change at hand. Some say that people resist only change imposed on them. Under any circumstance, an act or effort to change, be it individual or collective, requires three successive steps: awareness, practice, and persistence.

AWARENESS

The first step is a recognition that something must change or is changing. Awareness is instigated by courage. Courage is a capacity to act in situations with unknown futures or assurances that desired outcomes will be achieved. Courage has its roots in a conviction that the matter at hand is important and needs to be addressed.

Whether it's looking in the mirror and admitting that we're fat and need to lose weight or recognizing that our position needs to cede or adapt to those with more understanding, influence, authority, or power, we start by acknowledging that things need to change (or are changing), either the kind of change that we effect or the kind that happens to us. Change can be daunting, and arguably, getting started may be the most difficult part.

PRACTICE

For many or most things, change—that is, replacing or modifying some behaviors or ways of thinking with others—takes practice. And just as courage helps awareness, humility helps practice. Humility helps set an attitude that change won't necessarily come easily or quickly, and strength can come from failure.

Norman Lear, a creative genius and icon in the television industry, once said, "Wherever I've stumbled, I found gold." Humility helps patience and persistence prevail, and this happens through practice. A buddy that I used to windsurf with would say that windsurfing is an activity of a thousand failures. One falls a lot before figuring out how to stand, which is to say that the path to change can be uncomfortable because of setbacks. But with persistence, setbacks can be overcome, and change can be durable.

PERSISTENCE

Persistence is about commitment and perseverance. It's about buoyancy and the ability to bounce back when knocked down. It takes time, particularly to break old habits and create new ones. Stephen Covey wrote in *Seven Habits of Highly Effective People* that, after 30 days, a new behavior becomes a habit.[3]

My experience says that's a bit optimistic. As Mark Twain said about stopping cigarette smoking, "It's easy. I've done it many times." All of this is to say that change is possible but not necessarily easy to achieve. The demands and constraints of the COVID-19 pandemic seem to have suggested that people have limits with their ability to change.

---

3 Stephen Covey, *Seven Habits of Highly Effective People* (FranklinCovey, 1989).

Just as courage is needed for awareness and humility for practice, commitment is needed for persistence. Courage, humility, and commitment—those are the magical ingredients to sustain successful change: the courage to figure out what needs to be done, the humility to understand that the change is challenge-worthy, and the commitment to stick with it, bounce back from setbacks, and try again.

More often than not, our behavioral choices lie on a continuum between opposites. For example, compare the advice to "look before you leap"—meaning be careful, don't be rash—with the aphorism "he who hesitates is lost"—meaning be quick, don't overthink. At both of these extremes, the ends are mutually exclusive, meaning you can't do them both. Likewise, acting your way into a new way of thinking and thinking your way into a new way of acting are opposite approaches; you can't do them both. The leadership quest is to discover and maintain an appropriate balance between these two extremes.

Courage and Cynicism

Two attitudes toward change—courage and cynicism—tend to either move people and organizations toward or away from embracing change.

Courage is the ability and willingness to act in a situation without knowing how things are going to turn out, without the assurance that desired outcomes will be achieved. It's about putting personal beliefs ahead of personal welfare. Courage is about being daring, bold, and resilient. Courage is what keeps us from quitting—or, worse, stagnating and not growing.

Cynicism is the despicable dark side of the equation. Cynicism has its roots in a reality that is perceived and described differently from the way others—friends, colleagues, leaders, the media, etc.—describe it. Among other things, pervasive cynicism creates conspiracy thinking and gaslighting, trying to convince people of things that simply are not true.

On the other hand, courage feeds resilience. The more courage we have, the more resilient we are in bouncing back from setback and driving change. The more cynicism we have, the more likely it is that we won't influence others effectively. These attitudes greatly influence anybody engaged in change, especially leaders.

Reflection

- Are you prone to adopt attitudes of courage or those of cynicism?
- What keeps you in appropriate balance?

In polarized times, it's easy to find others who describe reality in ways different from how you experience it, and that's true for everybody. An iconic example of this phenomenon is in the US media: Fox News and CNN. They're both describing different features of reality, and depending on whose "facts" you like or believe in, there are always people on the other side who describe and interpret reality very differently.

A consequence of ongoing polarization and cynicism in the workplace is that work culture can become toxic with pressures and conflicts that impact constituents differently. Effective leaders know how their constituents react and respond to change. Some will lead, and some will hesitate or resist. Good leaders know how to influence all of them, differently as needed, to help move the organization forward.

A senior executive I know in a multibillion-dollar global company advised his core team that the company's culture had changed. "We are no longer family. First and foremost, we must take care of ourselves." The executive perceived that long-standing features of the company's culture, unity and helpfulness, had changed, weakened, or been abandoned, primarily because of abrupt leadership changes at the very top of the organization and unanticipated stalled business growth. His response was to encourage his team to shorten their horizons and take care of matters closer to home at the business's core. When matters change for the worse, effective leaders shift their view and focus on matters of most strategic consequence.

As we all know, leaders and constituents leave organizations when they change for the worse—even if it doesn't happen all at once.

Workers Seek Purpose and Flexibility

The *Great Resignation* was coined in 2021 by Anthony Klotz, a professor at University College London's School of

Management, when he described the sustained mass exodus of employees from their jobs in the middle of the COVID-19 outbreak. When the pandemic hit in 2020, unemployment rates increased because of layoffs and businesses shuttering.[4]

However, in 2021, despite continued labor shortages, employees continued to leave their jobs. One theory is that the pandemic allowed workers to rethink their careers, work conditions, and long-term goals. Of necessity, the pandemic introduced workers to remote work. In 2022, while many office environments reopened, workers continued to be attracted to opportunities of remote work, because remote work affords schedule flexibility and the possibility of better work–life balance. As a result, leaders are more pressed than ever to provide purposeful work in optimistic environments where trust and integrity are strong.

Years ago, I consulted with a senior executive at a large multinational company. He was an amazing man. The company recognized his talent and abilities by giving him responsibility for two of the company's six business groups, something that had never been done before, having one executive run two separate businesses simultaneously. In addition to being a stellar executive, he was a Renaissance man. Among other talents, he painted, played classical music, and was an excellent skier. At the relatively young age of 55, he retired. When I asked him why he was retiring so early, he explained that if he kept working, he wouldn't be

4 Ann Kellet, "The Texas A&M Professor Who Predicted the Great Resignation," Texas A&M University Division of Marketing and Communications, February 11, 2022.

able to enjoy and accomplish so many other things that he wanted to do. To me, that's the personification of balance.

Reflection

- How are courage and cynicism expressed in your organization? How do you manage them?
- Do you pay attention to the flow of employees leaving your organization?
- If so, do you have a sense of why they're leaving?
- What are you doing to identify and keep the valuable employees that you want to retain?

Effective Leaders

Replacing effective employees can be expensive and time-consuming. Effective leaders pay attention to supporting and repairing relationships with valuable constituents. They reenroll their constituents and grow them to become accomplished leaders as well.

Effective leaders set a tone and largely influence their organization's culture simply by what they pay attention to and how they behave. A leader's challenge is to establish a path forward that reflects the desires and interests of their constituents as well as themselves. Effective leaders reach out as much as possible and elicit views from many people in their orbits.

I supported a senior executive for a while who ran a multibillion-dollar business with five divisions, all headquartered in the same place. Soon after he got there, he established a monthly meeting with a standard format that always began with employee acknowledgements, followed by a rotating spotlight on issues and developments. Sometimes, guest speakers addressed the audience as well. That was followed by a Q&A session, and then the meeting closed.

Over a relatively short period of time, attendance at the monthly meetings grew, and division leaders proposed and developed issues, challenges, and success stories to share at the monthly meetings. The meetings created an energy and alignment across the entire organization, and it took only the leader's doing to develop, orchestrate, and implement this practice. Sometimes it's inertia rather than resistance that stifles change.

Timing and Planning

Time often complicates and confounds a leader's challenge to process and respond to information and situations—that is, to lead. Sometimes leaders need time, reflection, and consultation to figure out how to navigate through complex matters and determine what to do next. Other times, typically in emergencies, leaders need to be instinctive and act rapidly. Effective leaders understand how to manage changes they can control and adapt to those they can't.

It is said that *plans are useless, but planning is essential.* The story of Osama bin Laden's capture perfectly illustrates that age-old adage. Extensive planning and practice preceded bin

Laden's actual capture. A replica of the building bin Laden was believed to be living in was built in the Nevada desert, and those selected to execute the mission practiced there for quite some time.

Once they were in Baghdad, the plan was to fly choppers over the compound and have SEAL team members descend from ropes into or near the target building. But things went wrong immediately. The fences surrounding the mock compound in Nevada were chain-link, allowing the chopper winds to flow through them. But in Afghanistan, the rescue team encountered solid compound walls that blocked the wind from escaping.

As a result, the choppers were forced to land inside the compound. One chopper crashed and needed to be destroyed before the SEAL team left, but as the world knows, notwithstanding that substantial stumble at the very outset of the mission, the team adjusted and executed the mission successfully.

The old adage that *plans rarely survive their first contact with reality* also proved to be true in the bin Laden raid, but the team's preparedness and ability to adjust rather than start over proved to be what they needed to be successful. Planning in this instance proved to be priceless.

Implementing Change

The national change initiative for nationwide COVID-19 vaccination vividly illustrated the challenges and complexities of implementing wide-scale change. Science suggests that vaccinations are the best way to beat, or at least contain, COVID-19.

But, clearly, not everybody agreed. Some, influenced by science, got vaccinated, while others proposed different solutions that they believed were safer or more effective. Then there were those who simply didn't want to get vaccinated for personal reasons. Propagating misinformation and promoting fear were two effective methods that influenced people to turn away from science and not get vaccinated.

As time went on, however, more and more people chose to get vaccinated. In this example, as in all cases of wide-scale change, there are always early adopters, fast followers, slow followers, and resistors.

The story of COVID-19 vaccination and remote work presents us with a national case study on leading change. To convince people to get vaccinated, the government and some agencies provided incentives. Then came mandates, from government entities and also from employers and public venues.

I think everybody would agree that each approach met with mixed results at best, and it wasn't entirely obvious that one approach was superior to another. Messaging was not clear and consistent over time.

Even at the time of this book's writing, organizations continue to grapple with policies about where people should work: at the office, at home, or in some hybrid version of the two. Many factors influenced those decisions, not least of which is organizational culture.

A Metaphor for Change

Years ago, I was with a friend in a bakery. When it was his turn, he pointed to the items he wanted and said to the server, "Let me have two or three of those rolls." After putting the second roll in the bag, the server looked at him and said, "So what's it gonna be—two or three rolls?" This story illustrates how critical it is to lead with precision and clarity if you want to achieve a successful outcome.

At its core, change is about stopping certain behaviors and starting new ones and about stopping certain ways of thinking and starting new ones. Using altitude as a metaphor, let's say ground level represents the actual behaviors and skills that need to change. Descending from higher altitudes, 30,000 feet could represent thoughts, ideas, concepts, theories, and models, and at 15,000 feet, patterns of behavior and logic can be described and identified.

Ultimately, ground-level behaviors explain and encourage desired behavioral change. This kind of gradual approach to leading change can help people better understand, explain, support, and prepare for needed changes and mitigate resistance to them.

CHAPTER 3

The Dynamics of Leadership

I remember in one of my workshops somebody making the case that they weren't a leader because they didn't have direct reports. And somebody else in the room said, "Well, that's absolutely not true because people listen to what you say. People respect what you think." The story is a good reminder that, ultimately, leadership is about influence.

Reflection

- Who are your favorite leaders and why?

continued

- How do they influence you?
- How do they motivate you?

On one hand, leaders are forceful and express deep conviction that what they believe is important. At the same time, they have empathy and are not overbearing. They build trusting relationships that bolster confidence and encourage their constituents to step up to challenges.

Leadership Is an Influence Relationship

Dwight Eisenhower said, "Leadership is about getting people to do what you want them to do because they want to do it." It's about influencing people in one direction or another, and it's about relationships because it's about the dynamics between leaders and constituents.

Leadership is an influence relationship among leaders and constituents who intend real changes that reflect their mutual purposes. The genius of leadership lies in the ways leaders see and act on the exchanges between themselves and their constituents. They bring genius to a range of opportunities that help them engage and connect with constituents to build trust around common goals. That is the heart of leadership.

Effective leaders understand that their job is to influence constituents around matters that are real for all of them. A leader's best tools for building influence are the elements of integrity, telling the truth, keeping promises, admitting mistakes, and doing what's best for the larger organization. Leaders with integrity gain commitment and support from constituents and create trusting cultures for their organizations.

The pandemic-driven resistance about masking and vaxxing mandates underscored how difficult it can be to lead change. Effectiveness seems to be less about leaders telling their constituents what they need to know and do and more about capturing their constituents' imaginations and driving change around matters that are very real to them.

Navigating successfully through change can be complex. Sometimes there is a clear sense of where the organization needs to go, and the leader's challenge is to assemble a team with the needed skill sets and to influence them to want to go there also. At other times, change is happening, and the organization has no choice but to adapt and execute. In the first example, change is an aspiration. In the second example, change is a survival mandate. In either case, and in any number of other scenarios of change, leaders need to discover ways to help their constituents move from where they are to someplace new, which at ground level, really means helping them stop ways of thinking and behaving and start new ones.

I once consulted with an organization that, at that time, was undertaking a major policy change regarding vacation accrual. The old policy, the one that was being abandoned, allowed employees to accrue unlimited vacation time. Some long-standing employees had accrued months of vacation time and held it until retirement and then got paid for it and retired early. The new policy insisted that employees use their vacation time in the calendar year in which it was earned.

As you can imagine, the first year that the new policy was implemented, some employees were taking more vacation days than they were working. During that first year, the policy in practice created a lot of chaos and work coverage challenges. The pain and disruption of that change were substantial, but leadership's judgement was that the disruption of the policy's first year of implementation was worth it; they preferred getting it behind them rather than gradually implementing the policy change over time. The organization's leaders decided it was better to rip the bandage off quickly and endure short-term pain than to remove the bandage gradually to avoid the ongoing disruptions and discomfort of drawn-out (and often unpredictable) change.

Know Yourself; Know Your Constituents

Georges Braque said, "The only thing that matters in art is the part that can't be explained." A cooking recipe typically includes specific ingredients measured to specified amounts and prepared in certain ways. That's the formula. That's the algorithm. And the art of the recipe is "season to taste." A chef may season the same dish differently for different customers. In the art of leadership, "season to taste" means discovering ways to provoke and influence people in ways other than by coercion or intimidation.

When Eisenhower said, "Leadership is about getting people to do what you want them to do because they want to do it," he showed that removing coercion can help people get to the point where their motivations are internalized—and that's the nonrational side of leadership. It's not just logic and mechanics. That's the art of leadership.

The core prescription for effective leadership is to know yourself, know your constituents, and discover common interests. The better you know your constituents, the better you understand their values and motivations—their wants and needs—the easier it will be to discover effective ways to influence them.

It's important to understand constituents' perspectives about the organization's goals, culture, and history. The better leaders understand their constituents and their histories, the easier it is to determine what to do next—that is, how to lead them.

Effective leaders understand that they need to meet their constituents where they are before hoping to move them someplace else. Constituents embrace and support leaders who respect them; this is a prerequisite to understanding and supporting what needs to change.

Wants and Needs

Effective leaders get their people to act on objectives, matters, and achievements that are collectively shared. The deepest motivations lie in values, a collection of attributes that have importance, merit, and usefulness. Values-anchored motivations are best because values are typically deeply embedded. They change slowly if at all. A commitment to shared values aligns a group as no other motivation can. As far as possible, effective leaders use the larger organization's brand and reputation to leverage this effort. Arguably, values are from the heart; they are very personal.

People are also motivated by needs and expectations, as well as by wants and aspirations. These motivations are rooted in the future, a preferred future that addresses the needs and wants of both leaders and their constituents. At one level, needs and wants are subjective. What a constituent thinks is a need, a leader may think is a want or vice versa. Effective leaders understand their constituents' needs and wants and their associated priorities and expectations for success.

Sometimes negative examples can illustrate and provide learning opportunities about leadership effectiveness. I once knew a leader who, unfortunately, was a case study for what not to do as an organization leader, especially a new one. He enjoyed tremendous success throughout his career as a business leader. But in his last position before retirement, he was assigned a staff organization to lead, and he didn't make the time to get to know his team members to better understand their capabilities and motivations for work before he implemented his new agenda.

One of the most dramatic changes he made was implementing a mandatory all-day meeting every Monday. It quickly became apparent to all but him that spending one full workday per week to lead the organization was excessive, unnecessary, and not a productive use of anyone's time. His team's resentment grew and reached a breaking point, and so they appealed to their leader's leader to intervene. It was difficult for everybody. The consequences of his failed leadership behavior were explained to him, and he was persuaded to accept a package and immediately retired.

This story provides many insights about leadership effectiveness. Understanding and considering what constituents want and need are instrumental to driving needed change. Selfishness and self-centeredness place substantial limits on effective leadership. The earlier such tendencies are identified, the easier it is to correct them.

The old adage *You can't teach an old dog new tricks* may be applicable, and appointing leaders to new assignments and arguably keeping existing leaders in place longer than what's best for them and the organization are consequential responsibilities on the shoulders of leaders.

Reflection

- How well do you know your constituents' needs and wants?
- How effective are you at influencing those matters?
- What else or what more could you be doing?
- In what ways are your constituents' needs also your own?

Effective leaders adjust their focus to accommodate what they think their constituents can adapt to with little stress or disruption.

The Genius of Leadership

The genius of leadership lies in the way effective leaders see and act on their exchanges with their constituents. Effective leaders can be resolute about what needs to be accomplished and, at the same time, open to hearing from constituents about how to achieve that. Effective leaders are particularly mindful and conduct meetings that afford opportunities to engage with and influence many constituents at the same time.

In May 1961, President Kennedy said, "I believe that this nation should commit itself to achieving the goal, before this decade is out, of landing a man on the Moon and returning him safely to Earth." And on July 20, 1969, Neil Armstrong and Buzz Aldrin became the first humans to walk on the moon. The genius of JFK's words in 1961 focused a nation to achieve that very daunting goal. On a much smaller scale, leaders engage in acts of genius all the time to build support and gain influence from constituents for shared visions and goals.

Years ago, one of my clients had grown increasingly agitated with his team's habit of multitasking during team meetings. Often, they were attending to email and other online matters while my client's meetings were in progress. He addressed the matter directly with the group and even implemented rules for computer use during meetings, but many ignored the rules and continued to conduct online business during meetings.

To get everybody's attention, he decided to make his point in a dramatic way. He asked one team member to be his ally and attend the meeting with a broken laptop, one that was ready to be replaced. He instructed his ally to appear to be working on his computer during the meeting. At a planned moment, the leader appeared to have snapped. He started yelling at his ally and abruptly grabbed his laptop and threw it forcefully against the wall and shattered it. Well, as you can imagine, this got everyone's attention. The leader allowed a moment for the event to sink in, then thanked his coconspirator for helping him make a point.

You might think this story contradicts my earlier description of the art of leadership as avoiding coercion and intimidation. But when influence and persuasion fail, you may—rarely, safely, and only when necessary—have no other option. This leader attempted several opportunities to influence and persuade, and only after those efforts failed, he resorted to coercion and intimidation. Although the act was shocking, that was the point. The leader didn't harm anyone, and he immediately made it clear that this was a planned demonstration and not a genuine violent outburst.

Sometimes a leader's genius takes the form of dramatic action rather than words, especially when they have forums (meetings) to address their constituents simultaneously. It's not clear to me how far and long that story traveled, but anecdotal data reported to me suggested that multitasking behavior during those meetings stopped. Was it genius? You decide. But it's indisputable that the leader's behavior influenced his constituents in ways he wanted. There are many acts of genius between JFK's galvanizing vision and my former client's dramatization that leaders sometimes do.

Reflection

- Think back to times when you got your constituents to do what you wanted them to do because they wanted to do it. What were those acts of genius?
- What creative means have you used to get your points across?
- What approaches–conventional and novel–can you take regarding current opportunities to influence your constituents?

Understand Your Constituents

Relationships between leaders and constituents are most successful (productive and harmonious) when they share common objectives and employ processes that create agreement—or at least help build consensus. As always, the leader is challenged to discover and sustain an appropriate balance between command and control on one end and influence and persuasion on the other and between demanding adherence and building alignment.

Effective leaders work to understand and appreciate their constituents—what's important to them and what assistance they need or would appreciate. They tolerate and even encourage constituents to voice contrary opinions. This helps them understand their constituents' motivations and develop ways to build trust. It also helps them assess leadership potential in others and determine how best to develop them. William Blake said, "Opposition is true friendship."

Effective leaders consider their constituents' capabilities and frame challenges in ways that stretch those capabilities but stop short of snapping them.

I have a long-standing relationship with a client who, through the years, has become more of a colleague. She has a people-first orientation to leading her business—the North American subsidiaries of a global materials manufacturing company—and lives that value as an integral part of how she leads. Through the years, she has taught me many effective leadership practices, two of which are best practices for stretching but not snapping. It's important to set expectations that are not impossible to meet. Some leaders, in displays of ego or to impress their boss, promise more than they can deliver—and that never ends well. At the extreme, those leaders leave.

My client knows her business and people very well and routinely meets with them individually to review and adjust their expectations as necessary. She works hard at helping her constituents commit to realistic and aggressive goals. She routinely reviews and adjusts expectations that stretch people but doesn't commit them to unachievable goals.

Her second leadership practice is about the art of sharing news about poor performance. As she explains it, while everybody needs to have a good understanding of business conditions and forecasts, some people need greater detail and more discussion than others. Effective leaders balance disclosing accurate business conditions while stopping short of creating panic and distraction.

Through years of experience, she has come to understand that, at levels with lower responsibility, individuals receive feedback that they are or have been falling short of their individual expectations better than when they receive news that business is in decline. The latter induces despair. For people not responsible for an organization's results, even if the business is in decline, that level of detail is unhelpful and therefore unnecessary.

I have known this client for many years, and I know that her instincts and abilities emanate from values developed long before she started working. Having leadership practices rooted in deeply held values helps drive the quality and consistency of leader–constituent interactions.

The Value of Being Clear

The clearer a leader is about what matters, the easier it is to lead. Effective leaders configure and expand a broader common denominator for themselves and their constituents to help build inclusivity in the organization. These practices all contribute to helping leaders understand both what is and what needs to be common to all group members and, alternatively, what should be more individualized and tailored to people's responsibilities, motivations, and abilities.

Effective leaders are clear about who the group is and, even more important, about what the group's collective purpose is. The clearer leaders are about their group's collective purpose, the easier it is for them to lead effectively. Leading is never easy, but knowing constituents well makes it easier for leaders to understand and decide what the right things to do are. The art of leadership often comes down to those choices.

Effective leaders lay bare what's important to them and to the organization. From formal organizational policies like documents posted for all to see to informal traditions like monthly birthday celebrations, most such practices pivot around prescriptions for accommodations and assimilations. Some things are to be tolerated and encouraged, while others are rules everyone must follow. It's important to clarify the difference between what's acceptable and what's not.

For example, rituals like birthday lunches once a month or happy hour Fridays are practices that organization members are encouraged but not required to join. At the same time, those very same organizations have policies and procedures that demand prompt and accurate execution.

For example, some organizations require after-action reviews. After-action reviews can take many forms, but what they all have in common are detailed and rigorous processes by which a team's past performance is evaluated. After-action reviews are often mandatory, rather than optional.

Be Decisive

The utility of leadership is decisiveness, focus, and activity. Leadership is not a critical need when what needs to be done is obvious. However, when what needs to be done is not clear, leadership provides tremendous value. The utility of leadership is describing and implementing a path forward when that path is not clear. Leadership brings clarity and precision to uncertainty. The utility of leadership gets people to uncover and discover what needs to be done and then do that.

The horrific events that happened in Uvalde, Texas, on May 24, 2022, are a tragic example of what can happen when leadership doesn't know and doesn't communicate what needs to be done. It was reported that many armed police officers were just outside of the classroom where a shooter killed 19 students and 2 teachers. It was reported that the officers waited 77 minutes before entering the classroom because nobody in charge gave the order to enter the classroom before that time.

Action is a bias that leaders must possess. Regardless of circumstance, leaders don't have the option of inaction—acting like deer frozen in the headlights—so even when they don't know what to do, they must decide. The Uvalde tragedy is a painful reminder of how inaction can be blamed on uncertainty.

CHAPTER 4

The Heart of the Matter Model

What gets you out of bed in the morning? What keeps you from just rolling over and going back to sleep? The answer is the heart of what motivates you. The Heart of the Matter model identifies core motivators that everybody shares. We're all motivated by a need for meaning, hope, and trust. That's what we need, especially from our leaders.

Within the first 30 minutes of my Heart of the Matter workshop, I ask participants to reflect on the reasons they get out of bed each morning rather than roll over and go back to sleep. I then tell them my answer: Each day, we need a sense of meaning, hope, and trust to accomplish our daily goals.

We all get out of bed each morning to further and deepen the meaning that work provides, to build confidence and hope that the work will have an impact, and to build and deepen trust with people at work. After explaining that, I check for sufficiency, whether anybody identified motivators that couldn't be subsumed under these three. That very rarely happens.

The Model

The Heart of the Matter presents a view of effective leadership in the form of a motivational framework to help people, individually and collectively, undertake endeavors for accomplishment. It connects motivation with outcomes.

You'll recall from earlier and see in Figure 4.1 that the model proposes that three core motivators move people to action: meaning, hope, and trust. These motivators share common characteristics. They are elemental; they're the lowest human common denominators. These motivators are also fundamental, important, and consequential. Finally, these motivators are foundational, with roots from which other ideas and actions grow.

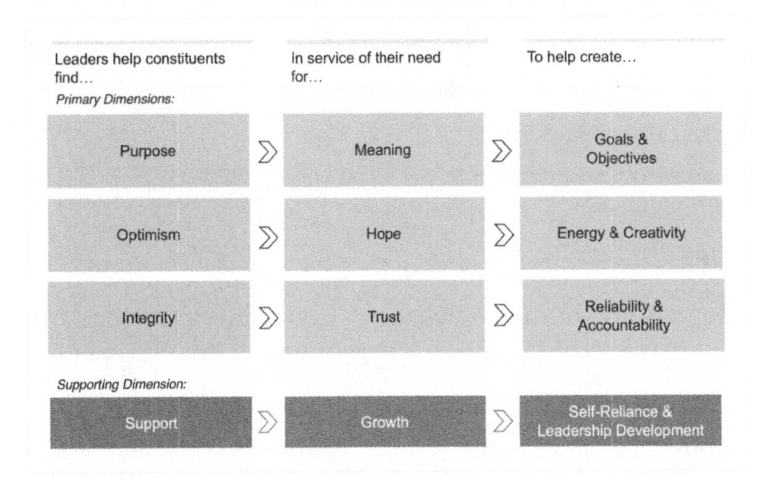

Figure 4.1

The Heart of the Matter model demonstrates how leaders help their constituents discover purpose, optimism, and integrity in response to their needs and wants for meaning, hope, and trust. These motivational pairs guide and influence important interactions and dynamics between leaders and their constituents. Constituents are motivated by meaningful work, and effective leaders help them discover work purposes in which personal meaning can be found.

MEANING

Although the model's motivators are not prioritized by importance, meaning is a good place to start. It explains why people do what they do. Meaning is a core motivational need that drives people and organizations to commitment.

Meaning lies at the intersection of values and responsibility. What people and organizations deeply believe and feel responsible for drive their creations and pursuits of visions, goals, and objectives.

HOPE

Hope is a core motivational need that drives the idea that what is desired can be accomplished. The prerequisite to hope is the need for goals, confidence about achieving them, and a pathway for getting things done. Without these prerequisites, it's not hope but simply a wish.

Hope also embodies resilience, the ability to bounce back from setbacks and failures, and self-efficacy, the belief that efforts have consequences—that constituents and leaders can and do effect the changes they want to achieve.

Everyone knows that work is always better (more productive with the right amount of stress) when it is infused with a sense of hope—a plan and a confidence that the plan can be achieved. Effective leaders convey confidence and optimism in ways that help their constituents become more hopeful, energized, and committed to their work challenges.

TRUST

Trust is a core motivator that assumes most if not all accomplishments worth pursuing need collaboration. This motivator is about relationships and how people link together to get things done. While meaning and hope can be generated from within, trust is a motivator that exists only between people.

Building and maintaining trust takes attention and effort. Trust is challenging to build and—unfortunately—too easy to destroy. Effective leaders model integrity in ways that help people trust them and become more trusting and trustworthy themselves.

Unpacking the Heart of the Matter Model

It's best to first unpack the Heart of the Matter model by column. The figure's left column describes the value-add of leadership and how effective leaders motivate and sustain quality work and relationships. The most effective leaders earn their constituents' respect with their integrity and guide rather than direct their constituents to their purpose and sources of optimism.

The middle column identifies the core motivators that constituents need to keep doing important work: meaning, hope, and trust. Effective leaders help their constituents discover and harness those motivators.

Finally, the right column explains the utility and payoffs of these leader–constituent interactions. Together, leaders and constituents create objectives that they can address with energy, enthusiasm, and creativity in reliable and accountable work environments.

The labels on the figure's 12 boxes are set and permanent, but the content of each box is influenced by specific leaders and constituents, along with their leadership challenges. Purpose and meaning, optimism and hope, and integrity and trust work together to create a group's effectiveness.

It's also important to explain what the figure does not represent. Although the columns and rows are portrayed separately and are distinct from one another, the concepts they represent are not independent of one another. They all mix together in real time. These dimensions interact through the ways leaders and their constituents design, implement, and execute plans for progress. However, to best describe and appreciate each core motivator, I explain them separately.

In addition to not being independent of one another these motivators are also not hierarchical. Although the figure lists meaning first, hope second, and trust third, that is not meant to convey any relative importance of these core motivators. It's not to say meaning is more important than trust, for example. Effective leadership needs to create, encourage, and support all three motivators—in balance—and to focus on whichever motivator needs more attention in any given moment.

VIEW THE FIGURE AS A FLOW CHART

The last thing to mention about the figure before examining each of its components more closely is that the figure should be viewed as a flow chart from left to right. The left column is the input: what leaders do to influence their constituents. The middle column is the throughput: how constituents use what they get from their leaders. And the right column is the output: what is produced and accomplished.

The Heart of the Matter's supporting dimension, shown in Figure 4.2, conveys the significance of developing leaders by providing support and opportunities for their need to grow. Effective leaders provide sustainability and continuity to the process of growing new leaders.

THE SUPPORTING DIMENSION

Figure 4.2

In the absence of this supporting dimension, organizations lose continuity and consistency over time. Effective leaders create and manage succession plans for future leaders and prepare for these up-and-coming leaders to develop.

Reflection

- How were you prepared for your current position?
- What aspects of that process do you or should you include, exclude, or add to help create your organization's next generation of leaders?
- Have you, as Henry Miller suggests, helped your constituents become better leaders by helping them believe in themselves?

continued

- What methods have you used or might you try to instill confidence in your team members?

Effective organizations constantly reinvent themselves, and they do so in large part by growing motivated leaders. At its core, the Heart of the Matter is about inspiring, motivating, and guiding focus. In the absence of focus, inertia sets in, putting the brakes on forward momentum. When the brakes are on and the focus is scattered, great things rarely get accomplished.

The Core Motivators

The model's three pairs of primary core motivators (see Figure 4.3)—meaning, hope, and trust—are best understood to flow and mix with each other in real time, making leadership the art that it is. This is not a mathematical model; it's fluid and subjective. These motivators are not independent of one another, and they're not prioritized by importance or any other factor. Meaning, hope, and trust are of equal importance, not prioritized; and they're mixed and changeable, not compartmentalized.

The Heart of the Matter Model

THE CORE MOTIVATORS

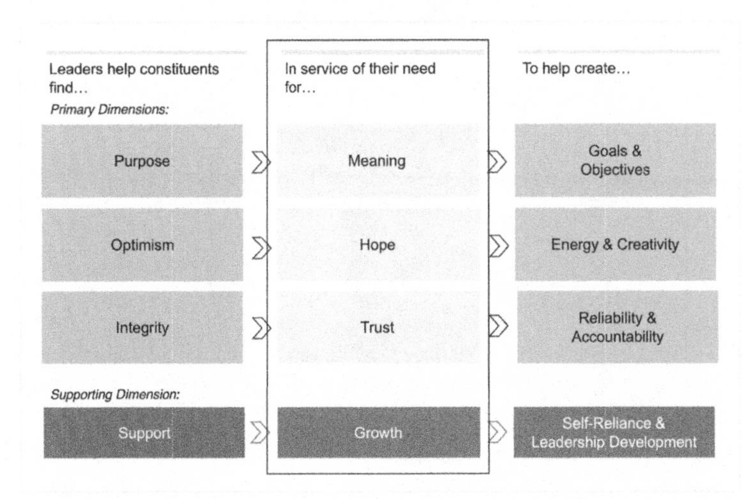

Figure 4.3

Each primary core motivator pair represents and characterizes aspects of leader–constituent interactions.

Looking at the figure by column, the left column describes what leaders provide (purpose, optimism, and integrity), answering the question, "What will help?" The middle column describes what constituents want and need (meaning, hope, and trust). Leaders help their constituents discover purpose for their sense of meaning. To do this, they demonstrate optimism and confidence that their constituents can, indeed, hope for the success of their efforts. Meanwhile, leaders also model integrity to help their constituents build trusting work relationships. The figure's right column, the outcome column, addresses the question, "What is gained?" The answer is outcomes, culture, and climate.

CHAPTER 5

Purpose + Meaning = Goals and Objectives

Meaning is a personal feeling, attitude, or belief that explains and gives value to what we do. The top row of this chart (Figure 5.1) shows how a leader can impact their constituent's purpose, which leads the constituent to discover meaning and ultimately helps them set their goals and objectives.

PURPOSE–MEANING–GOALS AND OBJECTIVES

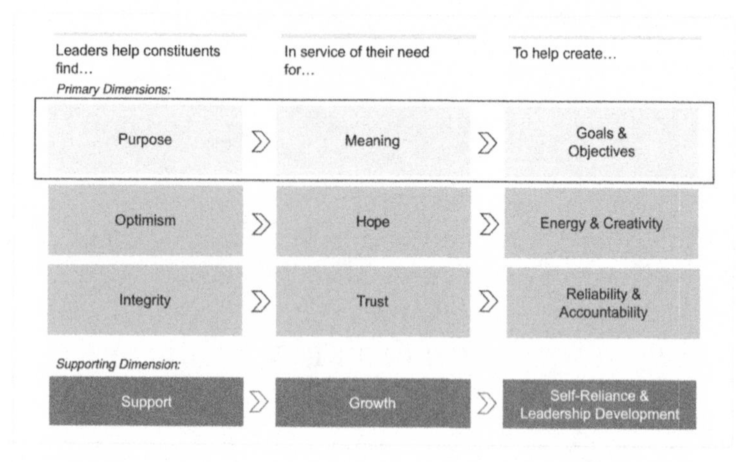

Figure 5.1

Purpose

Purpose represents a collective commitment to a preferred future, translated into goals and objectives that a group commits to achieving. A purpose is effective when it is anchored in strategy, influences organization objectives, and describes a preferred future. Purpose is about essence. Purpose cannot be motivated only by self-interest and opportunity. People (constituents) are motivated by a purpose that serves their personal need for meaningful work and helps motivate them to achieve important goals and objectives.

Purpose and meaning are ordered first in this figure because they are where every story about accomplishment begins. Decades of abundant research have established that meaningful work positively influences virtually everything.

When people believe they're doing meaningful work, their motivation, engagement, empowerment, job satisfaction, career development, individual performance, and personal fulfillment are substantially increased. Talk about a magic bullet! Purpose has it all.

In the Heart of the Matter, purpose represents a collective achievement to which a group is committed. Meaning represents something more personal. Meaningful work is what constituents want and need in order to thrive. The leader's responsibility is to help their constituents discover their sense of meaning and help them discover a larger purpose to which they can attach their individual sense of meaning.

Effective leaders help their constituents understand their jobs' objectives, goals, and purpose. Understanding one's job is first. What needs to be done? With whom am I collaborating? How much autonomy does this work encourage? What does it allow? Effective leaders help constituents shape the answers to those questions.

Groups create and share purpose, and individuals discover and attach their personal sense of meaning to that. Balance is achieved when individual personal meaning contributes to a larger, collectively supported purpose. The magic of this core motivation pair is the alignment it provides that helps everybody understand what the group is trying to achieve and their respective roles in making that happen. In balance, people know their responsibilities and are also able to execute them.

THE UTILITY OF PURPOSE

Purpose is an alignment tool; it clarifies priorities. Purpose brings stakeholders together, no matter how disparate or divided. Purpose can help reduce tension and create optimism and opportunities for growth. Purpose provides values-based ideals and accomplishments that all group members can understand and support and opportunities for group members to shape accomplishments through personal values and meaning.

Research has shown that people with purpose are more resilient in facing the stresses of everyday life. As Aaron Hurst put it forcefully and eloquently in *The Purpose Economy*, "People with purpose have more resilience to face the stresses of everyday life. People without purpose get stuck in the small details of everyday life and forget the larger goals."[5]

Purpose lives at the intersection of strategy, identity, and culture.

Strategy is about direction. Strategy is driven and shaped by vision, imagined but not yet realized, and points to a tangible and achievable future. Strategy engages purposeful work.

An example of this is Canon copiers, in the early years as they entered the copying business. They succinctly captured their strategy with the slogan "Beat Xerox." That unequivocally communicated what they were collectively aiming to accomplish.

---

5 Aaron Hurst, *The Purpose Economy: How Your Desire for Impact, Personal Growth and Community Is Changing the World* (Elevate Books, 2014).

Identity informs purpose and vice versa. A client I worked with a while back, in the relatively early days of the Information Age, once described his work this way: "I make computers safe for people." All these years later, I remember the passion and sincerity with which he said that. It was who he was, his authentic self. It was also at the heart of what the organization was trying to achieve.

A current-day example of identity is USAA, the insurance company that services military personnel, veterans, and their families. Who they are and what they do are inseparable.

The third ingredient that shapes purpose is culture, which I define here as a pattern of shared basic assumptions that are learned by members of a group. Culture helps groups solve their external problems of survival and also their internal problems of integration. An organization's culture helps group members learn the correct way to perceive, think, and feel about work life.

The Walt Disney Company is a good example of an organizational culture that does just that. The main characteristics of the Walt Disney Company's culture are innovation, quality, storytelling, and optimism, and those themes are and have been expressed throughout everything they do, and they influence employee motivation and behavior.

Strong cultures help constituents understand how they fit in. Effective leaders know their authentic selves and share this information in ways that help constituents understand the organization's reason for being and how they fit in. Effective leaders help shape constituent views of their membership and fit within the organization.

Reflection

- How important is what you do?
- If you weren't performing your job, what might happen? Would anyone miss you, or would the team carry on just fine without you?
- What might you do to ramp up your effectiveness so the answer to the above question can't be "No one would even realize I wasn't there"?
- Do you believe you fit in with your organization?
- If not, how could you make that change? How could you make others feel they fit in?
- How much autonomy do you have in doing that?

Cultural assumptions function to make work predictable and help reduce anxiety. The major dividend of a strong culture is that it stabilizes work life for group members. Culture is manifested by habituated rather than intentional behavior. What we do by habit reveals and reflects the collective values of a group's culture. Effective leaders help constituents align personal and organizational values and purpose. Purpose and conviction encourage and support resilience, and that's the ultimate utility of purpose: persistence.

The culture of the United States military in general, and each of the individual branches of the Armed Services in particular, saliently illustrates the value-add of a strong organizational culture. Whether you've served in the military or not, it's not difficult to observe the unifying nature of its culture.

I was once teaching a workshop on a university campus, and one of the participants was an Air Force major who was dressed in uniform. During one of our breaks, we were walking together on campus, and an Army private, also in uniform, crossed our path. When he saw the major, the private snapped to attention and saluted him. Uniforms are a widely understood designation of rank and achievement.

Meaningful Work

Viktor Frankl, an Austrian Holocaust survivor who developed logotherapy, based on the premise that a person's primary motivational force is to discover meaning in life, wrote "meaning grows out of identifying and devoting energies to those ideals, people, and activities for which you feel a sense of responsibility."[6] Common sense tells us that we feel most responsible for what we cherish and perceive as irreplaceable.

For me and no doubt for many others, the experience of parenting teaches this most powerfully. Children, especially newborns and infants, bring into sharp focus how dependent children are on parents or guardians for survival and

6 Viktor Frankl, *Man's Search for Meaning* (Boston: Beacon Press, 1962).

well-being. For some, pets may do that too. Being responsible for someone's or something's life is the ultimate manifestation of responsibility.

Meaningful work has three important features: It's significant and important, inherently fulfilling and rewarding, and a good fit between ability, interest, needs, and values. Work significance and importance are perceptions and beliefs held by others: Those who observe or benefit from the work are in this category. When a person feels their work is inherently fulfilling and rewarding, they are showing us what they believe about it. This is an internal feeling that is hard to detect as an outsider; we rely on our constituents to demonstrate how fulfilled they feel. The third criteria of a good fit contains both internal and external indices. Ability and interests are meant to be internal or personal perceptions and beliefs, whereas needs and values are more about organization and leader perceptions and beliefs. In other words, work is most meaningful when a person's abilities and interests fit well with their organization's needs and values.

FEELING VALUED

In my experience as a coach and consultant, I've observed that performance issues are often if not always mapped to individuals feeling insufficiently valued; whether by lack of compensation or recognition, these folks feel the nature of the work doesn't provide a sufficient feeling of accomplishment.

Or perhaps there's simply not a good enough fit between one's skill sets and those required by their work.

It only takes one of these features to be off or lacking for someone to feel their work is not meaningful. Sometimes a small crack can become a large chasm. Years ago, I worked with a law firm in which one of the partners felt insufficiently rewarded with challenging and important cases to work on, which he believed hampered his ability to advance in the firm. The matter was exacerbated by the managing partner's inability to convincingly explain this partner's contributions and limitations to him.

For the Heart of the Matter, responsibility and creativity are the forces that drive meaningful life and work. Meaning sits at the overlap of responsibility and creativity in service of worthwhile purpose. Meaningful work supports a sense of responsibility for work accomplishment and provides a venue and path for positive creative expression. Figure 5.2 illustrates these ideas. The figure shows the consequences of being in and out of balance and implicitly encourages being conscious of how time is spent. Effective leaders are mindful of how they spend their time.

I know a number of K–12 teachers whose work provides opportunities for both creative and responsible work. When I asked a special education teacher whether she would consider leaving the teaching profession to pursue other better-paying work, she said, "Who would take care of my kids?" That revealed to me a deeply embedded sense of responsibility to her students. At the same time, she regularly developed highly creative lesson plans that included storytelling and classroom decorations that helped illustrate the ideas she was trying to teach. That's an example of meaningful work.

WHERE MEANING COMES FROM

All meaningful work has two characteristics. First, meaningful work has its roots in responsibility. Meaning grows out of identifying and devoting energy and effort to ideals, people, and activities for which one feels a sense of responsibility, obligation, or duty. Sometimes, those obligations and duties are rooted in personal values, and at other times, they're rooted in commitments made to others.

The second characteristic has to do with creativity, the ability to imagine, invent, and express original and important ideas, talents, or visions. Efforts that afford those kinds of opportunities are meaningful.

Work that provides a high sense of responsibility and creativity is meaningful work. As Figure 5.2 shows, work that provides a high level of creativity but a low level of responsibility can be characterized as playful. That's a fun space to be in, right? Perhaps gamers live in this world. Networking and volunteering through work could be other examples that don't demand a lot of responsibility but could provide opportunities for creativity.

Purpose + Meaning = Goals and Objectives

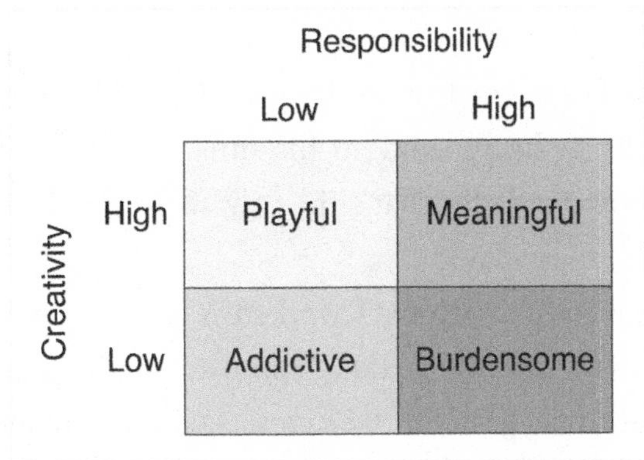

Figure 5.2 Distribute your time across these four quadrants.

When work provides high levels of responsibility but low levels of creativity, it can be stressful or burdensome. Such work provides substantial responsibility but little to no outlets for creative expression. Unfortunately, many people at work live in this world. I have one client whose sole opportunity to do creative work is helping customers solve problems. Working with customers brings her great joy. Unfortunately, her customer-focused time is overwhelmed with internal reports and presentations that her work requires. It demands much more responsibility than creativity.

Addictive work provides little to no responsibility or creativity, but it's done because we can't help ourselves. Workaholics spend a lot of time in this space. I well remember the man who ran the IT department at a company I once worked for who always had a game going on his computer. I don't recall what his game of choice was, but it was always up on his screen and he would turn his attention to it between those times that he was doing work. Effectively, he multitasked between work and his game. His time playing his game didn't seem to provide that much fun or demand his creativity. He seemed to do that simply to fill gaps between work tasks. I always think of his situation when I think of addictive work. Sadly, that's the way some people approach their work every day.

The location at which I worked was in a stunning setting. Access from the parking ramp to the building was a long, slightly inclined bridge across a wild greenbelt. While that provided a pleasant setting for entering and exiting the workplace, it also provided an opportunity to observe how different people came to work. Some people came with a bounce in their step; they walked with energy and purpose. They were getting somewhere because they had to accomplish important things. For other people, that walk was a slow approach to a predictable work environment that was, for any number of reasons, unattractive and unmotivating—useless bosses, untrustworthy peers, boring or meaningless work; the list goes on.

Workaholics are people who, unless they're eating or sleeping, are working. Some workaholics plow ahead even when the work is mundane or tedious. Often, this is because they're cleaning up somebody else's mess, have spineless leaders, or are disproportionately focused on the near term over the long term. At the other end, they're constantly working on things that need to get done. It's not necessarily that the work is meaningful or enjoyable but, rather, that it simply needs to get done—so they keep on working.

Reflection

Distribute 100% of your time across the four quadrants in Figure 5.2 (meaningful, playful, burdensome, and addictive):

- Are your allocations "just right"?
- If not, consider what you might do more of and less of.

MEANING AND WORK

Studs Terkel, a twentieth-century writer, historian, and broadcaster, wrote in his book *Working* that work was "about a search for daily meaning as well as daily bread, for recognition as well as cash, for astonishment rather than torpor—in short, for a sort of life rather than a Monday through Friday sort of dying."[7]

Work needs to be validating. Meaningful work is a positive ingredient and motivator. People need to feel good about what they do. They need to believe in what they do and understand their positive contribution. Research has demonstrated that people who have firsthand experience with recipients or beneficiaries of their work are much more motivated to work than those who don't have that connection.

---

7 Studs Terkel, *Working: People Talk About What They Do All Day and How They Feel About What They Do* (New York: Pantheon, 1974).

Reflection

Think of a time when you worked on something particularly meaningful.

- How was that experience unique and memorable?
- How did that experience make you feel?
- What aspects of that experience can be replicated in how you now work and lead?
- Can you do more to bring your constituents closer to their customers and clients?

Leadership is intimately and intuitively connected to promoting purpose and meaning in the workplace. Effective leaders have internalized judgement about what makes work worth doing.

I once asked workshop participants to create messages that convey their work's meaning to their employees. One participant explained that he managed a group of people whose jobs were to place ordered items in boxes, and he protested that it was impossible to bring meaning to work like that. Because the exercise was an evening homework assignment due the next day, all I could do was encourage him to keep thinking about it.

The next day, when it was time to report on the homework assignment, the manager who had challenged the value of the exercise eagerly volunteered to go first. He simply said, as if speaking to his employees, "Picture the look on your customers' faces when they opened the box you sent them and found everything they expected." The other workshop participants broke into spontaneous applause, and I knew right there and then that I'd have a great story to tell in subsequent workshops.

All work can have meaning. It's often simply a matter of perspective, and effective leaders help their constituents discover that. Leaders who help their constituents discover meaning at work are typically transparent, honest, and influenced most strongly by their values. Leaders driven by internal processes like values and beliefs are more effective in helping constituents discover meaning at work than leaders driven more by external processes like social expectations and rewards. Effective leaders enhance workforce commitment, satisfaction, meaningfulness, and engagement.

Reflection

- What's your balance between being driven by internal processes like values and beliefs and being driven by external processes like rewards and recognition?
- If you favor one over the other, why do you think that is? How does that benefit you? How does it hurt you?
- What can you do to bring better balance to this leadership orientation for you?

WORK ORIENTATION: A LENS TO PURPOSE

Work Orientation is a psychological construct that describes work disposition: internalized judgements about what makes work worth doing. The first motivational level of work orientation is a job orientation: This is the idea that we work to live. At this level, people are motivated to work to earn the means to acquire resources needed for living safely, securely, and comfortably. The next level in this hierarchy is a career orientation, looking beyond the basics of the current job to career progression, what's next and beyond. The highest level of work orientation is a calling, viewing work as integrating and expressing personal meaning and values.

CULTIVATING MEANINGFUL WORK

Meaningful work influences significant goals and objectives that recognize, inspire, and commit to achieve an organization's contributions. Ultimately, leaders are accountable for getting that work done.

Leaders help constituents understand their jobs, the outcomes of which contribute to the organization's collective purpose. Through this process, leaders help their constituents understand what they need to do and accomplish, how important that is, and the degree of autonomy and collaboration that work necessitates.

Leaders influence those outcomes and decisions. They help calibrate work's importance, and as needed, help their constituents understand how much autonomy they have. Leaders help their constituents understand how meaningful their work is by helping them understand work importance, contribution, and autonomy.

I once worked with an organization that implemented a substantial organizational change in which the division's leaders replaced the organization's hierarchical structure with a matrix. In matrix organizations, the business hierarchy is replaced with a collection of functional organization leaders like sales, marketing, etc. A strong argument for matrix organizations is that they are set up to drive decisions closer to where the matter occurs.

For matrix organizations to be effective, they need to be led by reasonable and open people who understand the interests and needs of the larger organization and then put those first. The leaders in this instance reasoned that, once the new workflows and accountabilities were settled and understood, the processes would run smoothly, and the exceptional ones that demanded management involvement would surface quickly and get attended to. It was a substantial change that affected many people's roles and responsibilities.

After more than a year, the matrix organization was dismantled and replaced with a modified hierarchical structure. In hindsight, while the organization's leaders meticulously engineered the matrix organization, they did not convincingly explain the structure's utility, and they captured very few of their constituents' hearts and minds. I sat with the organization's senior leader, and while he showed me a very complicated org chart of the matrix organization, he said, "The problem with this is that, when something goes wrong, I don't know who to squeeze."

Leaders bestow meaningful work via two primary means: role and membership. Role is essentially a position's design that details its needed skills, task significance, and autonomy. Membership, effectively managed, helps constituents feel included, which is a major building block for developing trust.

Leaders help create opportunities for their constituents to broaden and fortify the variety of needed skills for the job. They also help their constituents deepen their appreciation for the significance of their work and the boundaries of their autonomy. They often—if not always—also identify who constituents need to collaborate with and then connect them through assignments on work projects. They also invite their constituents to attend meetings about matters outside their existing scope of responsibilities to expose them to other organizational matters. Leaders also help define and explain which aspects of their work are theirs alone to control and which parts of their work demand collaboration and sharing with others.

A CEO of a large multinational company once told me that he knew a business was in trouble when the engineering team leaders would tell him what the sales organization needed to do and the sales team leaders would tell him what the engineering organization needed to do.

Leadership is about helping constituents manage their fit with the organization's culture, which is essentially about the fit and match between personal work orientation and the organization's culture. From the outset and throughout leader–constituent relationships, effective leaders help their constituents learn the culture and the subtle and nuanced matters that might otherwise be overlooked or missed.

I have one client who is talented at selecting, introducing, and establishing constituents in her organization. For her, it starts with the selection process. Among candidate assessments of qualification for any position, she includes an assessment of a candidate's fit with both the team's and the larger organizational culture. My client has eliminated otherwise qualified candidates for consideration based on judgements about that candidate's style, expressed beliefs, and values.

One of my clients has a practice at monthly meetings to have their organization members, independent of level or function, tell stories about cultural matters encountered in the previous month. At the outset of implementing this practice, the leader led with stories about matters pertaining to the organization's culture. The rest of the organization quickly picked up on the utility of sharing such stories and started contributing their own. The participants learned to avoid casting events in either a positive or negative light. They were shared to help everybody become more educated about diversity and inclusion.

A FEW GOOD MEN

The movie *A Few Good Men* illustrates how people can discover their way to meaning and purpose at work. Early in the movie, Lt. Daniel Kaffee (Tom Cruise) is selected to defend two marines accused of murdering a colleague. They maintained they were simply following orders from their commander, Colonel Nathan Jessep (Jack Nicholson), who was a highly regarded, tough, and fearless officer on a fast-track for greater responsibilities and a distinguished military career. Kaffee was selected for the job of defending the two marines because he had a well-established track record for settling cases and never bringing them to trial, which was just what was wanted of him—to keep Jessep's career unblemished.

Kaffee's superior officer, Lieutenant Commander JoAnne Galloway (Demi Moore), had a different view. She wanted Kaffee to demonstrate his untapped talents as a trial lawyer and, at the same time, let the two marines be judged.

To that point in Kaffee's career, he had never even been in a courtroom. Galloway was very confrontational with Kaffee in trying to persuade him not to settle and rather to bring the case to trial. She even suggested that his struggles with his father's high expectations of him were part of what kept him from engaging in trial work. After a heated argument with Galloway, Kaffee took time to reflect on the matter and eventually decided that the two marines needed their day in court. When the judge asked, "How do your clients plead?" Kaffee replied, "They're not guilty."

We can only surmise what changed Kaffee's mind. The movie never makes that crystal clear. It seems like, prior to his confrontation with Galloway, Kaffee's sense of meaning was efficiency: open and close cases as quickly as possible. Whether that sense of meaning was tied to any larger purpose is hard to say. Perhaps he felt a loyalty and obligation to abide strictly with the letter of the law for his military position.

Coupled with time to reflect, after the confrontation with Galloway, Kaffee's sense of meaning shifted from efficiency to advocacy, and what deepened that was that he chose to advocate both for his clients and for the process.

The critical leader in this story is Lieutenant Commander Galloway, because she held and imbued in Lt. Kaffee a larger purpose: the trial process representing the justice system based on facts and truth. Galloway successfully influenced Kaffee to embrace the larger purpose.

This movie provides a good example of what effective leaders do. They help their constituents discover their own sense of meaning and align it to their organization's greater purpose.

A STRONG SENSE OF VALUES

What makes leaders effective at influencing constituents to develop and align their sense of meaning at work with a larger purpose for which the organization stands, holds itself accountable, and guides its path forward? It begins with the leader having a deep sense of self, who they are, the values they hold dear, and what's important to them and the organization. With that, they are clear and communicative about their sense of purpose. They look for and take advantage of opportunities to share their sense of purpose with their constituents. They seek opportunities to test themselves to better understand the limits of their convictions and what they will and won't sacrifice for the organization. They develop their teachable point of view and let others know where they stand.

They don't assume that others share their sense of purpose, and they foster an environment that helps others discover their own sense of meaning. They do that in part by allowing and encouraging their constituents to explore alternatives, and they are mindful and careful not to lead by coercion and position power. They encourage questions and use reflective questions, such as "Why do you think that?" to get their constituents to examine their own underlying motivations. They resist offering solutions and answers. They ask more than tell. Effective leaders identify and promote shared purposes and values. They encourage and facilitate conversations and activities about shared interests.

Reflection

- How do you know that your goals and objectives are clear and commonly understood?
- How do you know that your constituents find them meaningful?
- Which practices from the final section on values are habitual for you? Which can you stand to strengthen and improve?

CHAPTER 6

Optimism + Hope = Energy and Creativity

Figure 6.1 explores the middle row of the Heart of the Matter model. It's very important to distinguish hope from false hope. Hope is extremely helpful. False hope is dangerous and destructive. Between February and October 2020, then president Trump repeatedly proclaimed that the COVID-19 virus was soon to be gone. He said, "We're turning the corner." However, during that period, 220,000 Americans died from the virus.

OPTIMISM—HOPE—ENERGY AND CREATIVITY

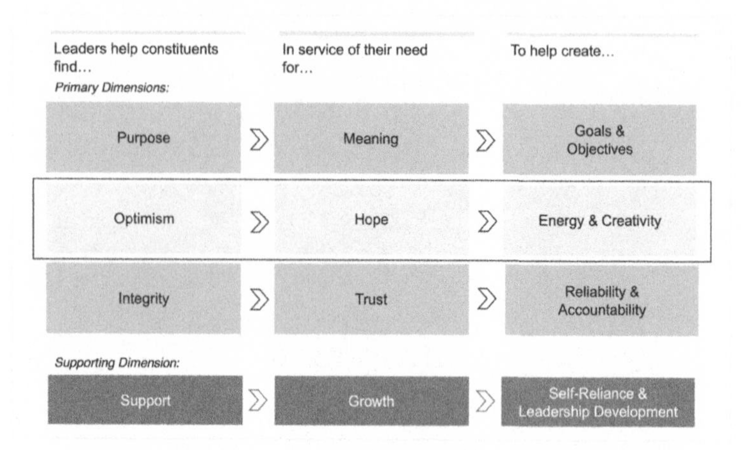

Figure 6.1

Subsequent to his statement, Trump explained that his job as president was to strike a hopeful tone to lift people's spirits and make them feel better. However, another view might see it as Trump perpetuating false hope, one consequence of which was leading some people to drop their guard (no masking, lax social distancing) while the virus was still active. Ultimately, everybody has their own assessment of leadership quality and virtue, so you decide: Was Trump's practice helpful? Was it ethical?

Hope is a motivational state that influences and drives goal-directed behavior. People who are hopeful don't give up. There's persistence in their drive. Most professional sports franchises—certainly those competing for a championship—express optimism throughout their campaign, as do most politicians running for elected office.

Hope contains three elements. Hope needs to be rooted in a goal; in the absence of a goal or purpose, there's really nothing to be hopeful for. The second part of hope is having the conviction that the goal is achievable. And the third element of hope is a pathway for achieving it. Hope embodies all three elements: a goal, a conviction, and a plan.

Reflection

- Think about a pressing goal or objective that you're in the middle of right now. How clear is your sense of your objective's desired outcome and pathway for getting there?
- How do the people you lead know about your confidence and convictions for specific achievements?
- What can you do to better align your team around their shared goals?
- How do you effectively and authentically cheerlead?

False Hope and Wishing

False hope is believing in something that doesn't have any basis for belief because the proposed goals are unrealistic or unarticulated. The quality and clarity of what is to be achieved, individually and collectively, influence pathways for success and confidence for accomplishment (getting things done). In the absence of compelling desired outcomes or objectives, confidence becomes detached at best because people lose sight of what's important; this is tied to purpose as well.

False hope is best exemplified by scams and scammers, people who contact strangers and propose opportunities that are too good to be true and, indeed, are not true. Scammers build false hope on false promises that gain people's confidence and ultimately extract money from them. The hope is false because the entire proposition they offer is nonexistent. But when scammers are successful, it's because they convinced their victims that they were telling—and selling—the truth.

Building false hope is always immoral and often illegal. Some people confuse or conflate hoping and wishing. Wishing is a passive state that demands no energy to make things happen. Some may say that deep religious conviction, prayer, and good deeds are expressions of hope, that they necessitate belief or faith, often in things that can't be controlled.

Hope and optimism are often connected to and expressed by persistence, the ability to confront failure and keep at it until getting it right. WD-40, the household product that stops squeaks, loosens rusted parts, and frees sticky mechanisms, is a great example of this. The 40 in its name represents the number of formulations it took its inventors to get it right.

Positive Psychology

There's a positive feedback loop between hoping and planning. Positive psychology has been a discipline within the field of psychology since 1998, when Martin Seligman chose it as the theme for his term as president of the American Psychological Association. Positive psychology contrasts with past practices in the field of psychology, which had tended to be focused on mental illness, maladaptive behavior, and negative thinking. Instead, positive psychology is focused on happiness, well-being, and positivity. It's the scientific study of strengths that enable individuals and communities to thrive. The field is founded on the belief that people want to lead meaningful and fulfilling lives and cultivate what is best within themselves.

Years of positive psychology research have identified four constructs: hope, self-efficacy, resilience, and optimism. In combination, these four constructs have a strong relationship with satisfaction and performance. They help explain the Heart of the Matter's core motivators of hope and optimism.

Let's examine these four constructs individually, with examples of how several businesses have met with success thanks to relying heavily on them.

HOPE

Hope is a feeling that accelerates activity, sparks creativity, and moves ideas to action. Hope is about having a goal, a conviction that it's worthwhile and achievable, and a plan for getting it done. Conviction is embedded in resilience, another core construct in the positive psychology framework.

The founding and growth of McDonald's is a great example of creativity and acceleration. Ray Kroc became famous and wealthy by introducing franchising and expansion to the company, but it was Richard and Maurice "Mac" McDonald who developed the transformative idea of fast service. They originally opened a drive-in barbecue and burger restaurant and shut it down after seven years of marginal success. They perceived that people were generally impatient and in a hurry, so they streamlined their menu to serve only burgers, French fries, and soft drinks and reopened their restaurant focused on a more efficient system of food preparation and delivery. The creative idea that people wanted quick service became the birth of this country's fast-food industry.

SELF-EFFICACY

How do people come to believe that they can produce desired effects by their actions? Albert Bandura, a distinguished scholar and educator who made substantial contributions to the field of social psychology, is acknowledged as having created the concept of self-efficacy. Bandura said, "Whatever other factors may serve as guides and motivators, they are rooted in a core belief that one can make a difference by one's actions. This core belief is the foundation of human motivation, performance accomplishments, and emotional well-being. Unless people believe they can produce desired effects by their actions, they have little incentive to undertake activities or to persevere in the face of difficulties."[8]

Self-efficacy is about believing in oneself. What one does makes a difference, and that's why what one does matters. Self-efficacy is an individual belief about a capacity to act in the ways necessary to reach specific goals. People who have a

8 See https://albertbandura.com.

strong sense of self-efficacy are motivated by outcome expectations and a belief in their ability to influence events that affect their lives.

Self-efficacy affects every area of human endeavor. By determining the beliefs a person holds regarding their power to affect situations, self-efficacy strongly influences the power a person has to face challenges competently. A strong sense of self-efficacy promotes human accomplishment and personal well-being. A person with high self-efficacy views challenges as things that are supposed to be mastered rather than threats to be avoided. These people can recover from failure faster and are more likely to attribute failure to a lack of effort or circumstances beyond their control. They approach threatening situations with the belief that they can control them. Strong self-efficacy has been linked to lower levels of stress and a lower vulnerability to depression.

In contrast, people with low self-efficacy view difficult tasks as personal threats and shy away from them. Difficult tasks lead them to reflect about skills they lack rather than the ones they have. It is easy for them to lose faith in their own abilities after a failure. Low self-efficacy can be linked to higher levels of stress and depression.

People with high self-efficacy carry and enjoy an element of certainty and confidence in their general demeanor. Effective leaders help their constituents recognize the positive effect of their effort and accomplishment. They help them realize and appreciate that the positive effects produced were a function of the actions they took to create them.

For a time, I worked with a senior leadership and organization development consultant and advisor. I spent a lot of time with him and learned a lot. One subtle thing he taught me was understanding the delicate balance between self-efficacy and hubris. I observed how he attracted clients and then worked with them. He had a large network of associates and colleagues, many of whom had complementary skills and experiences to do sophisticated consulting and coaching work in his client systems. He commanded respect because of his reputation and accomplishments, the confidence he generated, and the way he treated others.

When I was younger, I thought that, at times, his self-confidence expressed itself as arrogance, but now, reflecting on that relationship and partnership, I better appreciate how much good he did for his clients, colleagues, and collaborators, and how his confidence in himself contributed to his effectiveness.

RESILIENCE

Resilience helps us overcome setbacks that can get in the way of things working out well. Resilience helps us overcome stress, conflict, or failure. Everybody has a breaking point. Even the most resilient people can succumb to the pressures that surround what's trying to be accomplished.

The more resilient someone is, the easier it is for them to cope with setbacks. Resilience is a positive and effective way for coping with adversity or distress. Most people, especially in work environments, share or at least are familiar with common sources of adversity or distress. Stress and conflict are two very common setbacks people routinely experience.

Stress is an internal phenomenon, a physical or mental response to change and challenges. Stress, appropriately managed and balanced, is something resilient people handle well, and a well-managed stress level can contribute to productivity and accomplishment, as well as personal satisfaction and happiness.

Conflict is an external matter between parties. Underlying all conflict is a lack of understanding or agreement about what needs to be done or how something should be accomplished. Conflict impedes progress.

Resilient leaders recuperate from setbacks more quickly and even use setbacks to summon greater determination to pursue accomplishment. Stress and conflict are not the only sources of adversity or distress at work. Resilience helps overcome most work failures and changes. In general, resilience helps leaders recuperate, bounce back, and move forward. Resilient leaders don't quit. A dictionary definition of resilience is buoyancy—the phenomenon when a floating object is pushed down and when freed it pops back up. That's resilience.

Resilience is not unlimited or transferable from one situation to another. A story from the 2020 Summer Olympics (held in 2021 due to the COVID-19 pandemic) is instructive about resilience. At those Olympics, Simone Biles shared on social media that she was feeling burdened by the responsibilities she carried and that she felt affected by the pressure of the Olympics. She decided to put her mental health first and withdrew from the rest of the competition.[9] She said she was inspired by Naomi Osaka, who had withdrawn from the French Open and the Wimbledon Tennis Championships earlier in the year for similar reasons. The story shows the complex nature of resilience and how it may be more relative than absolute. The postscript to this story is that Simone Biles returned to competition in 2023 and won the world championship, becoming the most decorated gymnast of all time.

A rubber band illustrates an apt analogy for resilience. If it is stretched too far, the rubber band snaps. Effective leaders know how to stretch their constituents safely, stopping short of snapping them. These leaders know when and how to build and release tension for their constituents and their organizations.

The business world is abundant with examples of resilience. One is the story of Steve Jobs and Apple Computers. He formed the company with Steve Wozniak in 1976, and they successfully launched Apple II in 1977 and then experienced failure with Apple Lisa in 1977. After the Lisa failure in 1984, Jobs developed Macintosh, the first mass-produced computer with a GUI (graphical user interface). In 1987, he was kicked out of Apple and quickly started NeXT and then worked with George Lucas to create the animation company Pixar. He came back to Apple when they acquired Pixar and went on to save Apple from bankruptcy and to grow it to become the company it is today. Steve Jobs was a resilient leader.

9 See https://www.essence.com/celebrity/simone-biles-feeling-olympics-pressure-tokyo and https://www.nytimes.com/2021/07/28/sports/olympics/simone-biles-out.html.

OPTIMISM VERSUS CYNICISM

According to Martin Seligman, the founder of positive psychology, optimism is revealed by how people incorporate and respond to success and failure.[10] When optimists are successful, they tend to attribute that success to their own efforts; when they experience failure, they tend not to blame themselves. They may chalk it up to circumstances, or they may look at it as an opportunity to learn from a mistake or misfortune. Optimists don't own failure personally. But when something doesn't go right, the non-optimistic approach is to personalize the failure and attribute fault to oneself and one's team.

Some people in my workshops have objected to this perspective. They found it unattractive—too self-serving or selfish. But that's missing the point. I believe the point is that when positive events happen and you have some control over them, they happened because of what you did. Your positive attitude allowed you to see the opportunity rather than all the possible paths to failure. That's my sense of optimism.

Optimism is an attitude connected to good mood, perseverance, achievement, and physical health. Optimists believe they make good things happen; optimistic people are generally not grouchy. Optimists let other people know what they're excited about. They have elevator speeches and repeat them often. Good leaders are good storytellers. Telling stories—especially

---

10 Martin Seligman, *Learned Optimism: How to Change Your Mind and Your Life* (A.A. Knopf, 1990).

positive stories of success or overcoming obstacles—helps people understand context, and good examples are very instructive. The practice of being communicative helps leaders convince themselves as well as others. Good stories move matters and concepts from the abstract to the specific and tangible.

I once heard the CEO of a large and diversified company explain the strengths and strategy of his company in ways they'd never been explained before. He noted that the company had three key strengths. One was its robust international organization; the company had subsidiaries in over 50 countries. Another was technology; the company had a half dozen technology platforms from which it grew more than 60 distinct businesses. The third was manufacturing; the company made things. It had manufacturing facilities in North America, Europe, Asia, and Latin America. It knew how to build and run manufacturing plants.

These three strengths served as an umbrella that helped everybody understand what they did well and where they fit in. For much of his first year as CEO, he repeated this idea every time he addressed company leaders and employees. Part of this characterization of the company that made it so powerful was that none of his predecessors had ever described the company that way.

A few years ago, an executive vice president of a multibillion-dollar global business organization asked me to work with one of his division vice presidents. That person was brilliant. He had a lot of experience and was able to read people quickly and accurately. Unfortunately, he often expressed himself and his views with cynicism. That tendency often frustrated the people who worked for him and alienated him from his colleagues. Talent left his organization, and the executive team that he was a part of never became a high-performance executive team.

After a period of working with and coaching him, I judged that I couldn't help him change. His cynical attitude was too deeply rooted in his personality. I shared this with the executive vice president who'd invited me in to help. After a relatively short period of time, the vice president was asked to leave the organization.

The current state of partisan politics in the United States is a prime example of the impact of cynicism and the effect that's having on the country's institutions and the rule of law. Between accusations of a deep state, contested elections, conspiracy theorists, and fringe organizations like QAnon and the Oath Keepers, the country is becoming divided to its peril. There are too many pressing issues like climate change that demand immediate action, yet not nearly enough is getting done. The country's political parties continue to grow entrenched and unyielding. It feels like the prevailing view is that position is more important than purpose, and that puts the country's unity in jeopardy.

Everything ties back to being rooted in meaningful goals that provide excitement about achievement and confidence about progress. Spending time at the outset to develop and explain organizational goals is the first and critical step to success.

Reflection

- How well do you understand what you need to know to lead effectively?
- How can you improve your communications network?
- How well and appropriately do you disseminate information?
- How often do you or leaders you know claim ignorance after failures are revealed?
- In what way does claiming ignorance help you or them? How does it harm you or them?

A Powerful Story of Hope

The Shawshank Redemption, a 1994 film starring Tim Robbins as Andy Dufresne and Morgan Freeman as Ellis "Red" Redding, is a powerful story about despair and hope. As Andy explained, "Hope is a good thing, maybe the best of things, and no good thing ever dies."

Despite his claims of innocence, Andy was serving a life sentence for murdering his wife and her lover. Red was a contraband smuggler who had been imprisoned for many years and whose requests for parole had been repeatedly denied. In his own words, he was "an institutional man." Andy and Red developed a close relationship over two decades. But the men had different attitudes toward their positions. Red was resigned to life in prison. Andy was not.

Andy was an optimist and believed that he was an innocent man. He had a goal of freedom and developed—and executed—a plan to tunnel out of the prison through the painstaking process of removing small amounts of sand, bit by bit, so as not to draw attention to his work. He also made elaborate preparations for when he'd start life anew once he was out.

Andy never gave up. He wasn't going to spend his life in prison being punished for something he didn't do. Nothing superseded his goal for freedom. He had a plan. He spent years chipping away at making a hole in the wall of his cell that would eventually be his exit. He had to be careful to distribute the dirt he dug in small amounts so as not to draw attention to a growing mound of dirt. He did this by putting very small amounts of dirt in his pocket daily and then distributing it outside in the yard.

His discipline and conviction moved him methodically and steadily toward achieving his goal of freedom. There were so many opportunities to give up, so many opportunities to convince himself that the plan would not work. But he didn't let those negative thoughts in. He had it thoroughly thought through. He had a goal: freedom. He had a plan: to tunnel his way out. And he had a conviction: He could make that happen.

Perseverance

Remember, leadership is an influence relationship. Effective leaders recognize talent and understand how to influence effectively. They encourage perseverance by removing barriers and providing resources, support, encouragement, and incentives. Effective leaders help their constituents understand work's challenges and the rewards of success. Leaders help their constituents understand and avoid despair and the consequence of doing nothing or giving up. Effective leaders recognize and tap their constituents' key motivations and help them discover and develop new ones.

Perseverance is fueled by compelling goals and deep convictions that they are attainable and worthwhile. Athletes who sustained severe injuries and then submitted to challenging, rigorous, and lengthy rehab programs are prime examples of this behavior.

A story about Jerry Weintraub, an American film producer, talent manager, and promoter, always comes to mind as the quintessential example of perseverance. He told the story that one night he dreamed that the marque at Madison Square Garden advertised an Elvis Presley concert promoted by Weintraub. At that time, Presley was not yet doing concerts. But Weintraub called Colonel Tom Parker, Presley's manager, and told him that he wanted to promote a nationwide tour.

Parker dismissed the idea and declined the proposal. So starting the next day, Weintraub called Parker every morning at the same time with the same proposition over and over again. Weintraub continued to call Parker every morning for over a year. Finally, Parker agreed. Weintraub knew that promoting Presley would change his life, and it did.

Another example comes from a company that built perseverance into its culture. The creation of Post-it notes at

3M is but one example of persistence and ultimate triumph. Many companies, especially older ones, have stories like it. The Post-it story was that senior executives were not sold on the viability of the product, but the product advocates would not shut the project down before distributing samples to the company's executive assistants. It was these assistants' strong advocacy that saved the product. Back then I was interviewing a 3M executive who told me that he was concerned about the company's culture because product champions were not fighting back enough and were instead acquiescing too easily to executive vetoes of advancing new product development.

At the same time, effective leaders also exercise responsibility and help guide their constituents' efforts when longer-term impacts may be more dangerous than productive. Burnout is at the top of that list. Effective leaders *guide* more than they *direct* constituents to exercise good judgement.

When is it too much? What is the best time to throttle back or even back away completely? Effective leaders help their constituents discover that balance. And it's hard because we just never know for sure until something happens for good or for bad—and then we often say we should have realized that point before reaching it. Effective leaders help their constituents make those judgements.

A company executive client once told me that she's had sales managers call on accounts with new materials or data to try to convince customers to change their minds and buy from her company. On occasions, she had to intervene and stop a sales manager when those efforts became excessive and objectively showed no hope for persuading the customer.

Leaders help others see their limitations and motivations for themselves. An important Heart of the Matter message is that leaders often can't and shouldn't tell others what to do, but they can help others see more clearly. That is an example of the art of leadership.

Energy and Creativity

Energy is what gets us out of bed in the morning, right? Another day to engage in a fight worth fighting. And then the creativity piece goes to curiosity and persistence, and that's really where the rubber meets the road. Everything else is in our heads. But energy and creativity absolutely fuel the work.

Hopeful people working in supportive environments find work to be energizing, rather than draining. Effective leaders influence their constituents to discover confidence in themselves by providing opportunities for learning through work that both empowers and requires collaboration. They provide an appropriate balance of support and empowerment that helps explain the cause-and-effect relationship between what constituents do and the impact that they have.

Leaders help their constituents discover optimism by pointing out accomplishments they've already achieved. A while ago, I had a client who led a key account organization that had a dozen or so managers each assigned to a key account—customers who had sizable portfolios with the company or who were projected to grow into one. In some cases, the company manager resided at the customer's site to better understand

and serve their customers, manage their portfolios, and develop opportunities to grow those accounts further.

The leader did an excellent job of helping his people set stretch but achievable goals in each of those accounts. The leader also had the goal of keeping their key account managers focused on why they were there and preventing them from working to serve their customers' interests above their own. He guided them in this work by visiting often, bringing those key account managers back to the company offices, and reminding them about what they were there to do. Working with his key account managers, they set goals and reviewed progress regularly.

Energy and creativity reside in everyone, not just with the leaders and their leadership teams.

Prescriptions for Optimistic Leaders

In *The Shawshank Redemption*, Andy is self-led. Hope and optimism don't live in the world of problems; they live in the world of solutions. There will always be doubts, always someone who says, "This is what's wrong" and "This is whose fault it is" and "This is why these bad things are happening."

My message in the Heart of the Matter says that effective leaders are optimistic. They're focused on solutions—on what can and should be done.

Here are prescriptions for optimistic leaders:

- Be solution centered, not problem focused.

- Be entrepreneurial; look for opportunities.
- Be curious and consider a broad range of possibilities.
- Don't be easily satisfied.
- Be communicative.

Help people be steadfast. Help them resist quitting and push on. It all ties back to the beginning of the story of optimism. It is rooted in a conviction of a worthy (important) goal that is achievable.

Failure is not motivation to give up. Failure is motivation to keep tinkering until something better comes along.

Be intuitive. It's important to be very careful and mindful of self-fulfilling prophecies. Don't be driven by only the data. Sometimes one must look beyond the data to be hopeful.

We are all driven by whatever data we're reliant on. That data leads us to believe or to doubt. But hope is an intangible conviction that, in the face of things that might not seem that promising, we keep persisting. And the loftiness and importance of the goal makes all the difference.

CHAPTER 7

Integrity + Trust = Reliability and Accountability

The most animated and emotional participant exchanges in my Heart of the Matter workshops occur during the integrity–trust–self-reliance and leadership development sections (see Figure 7.1). I can't be certain why that is, but I think we tend to recall past experiences that were extremes one way or the other. We all have vivid (and in some cases indelible) memories of work environments in which trust was particularly high or low and in which people we worked with were exceptionally trustworthy and reliable or chronically suspect and unreliable. We remember those people because they had an outsized impact on our lives and well-being.

INTEGRITY—TRUST—RELIABILITY AND ACCOUNTABILITY

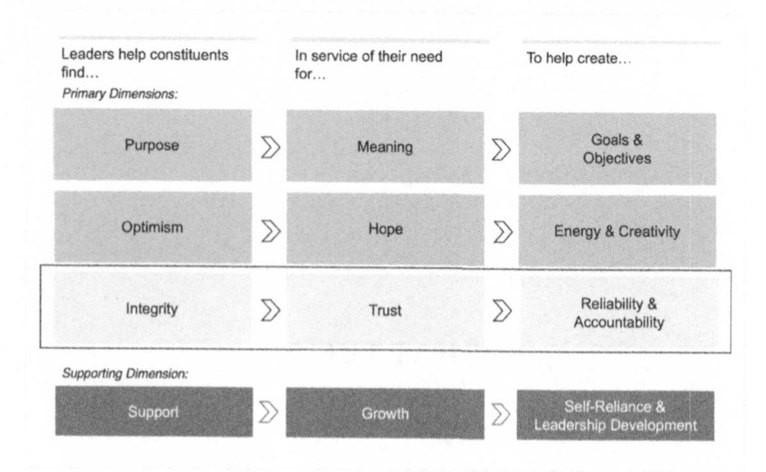

Figure 7.1

If pressed, we can discover meaning and hope without others' help, but trust and integrity can come about only between people. For this reason, trust and integrity are distinguishing features of the Heart of the Matter model and unique among the three core motivators. Nobody can discover their way to trust alone.

Trust

Trust, like confidence, is built on reason, but it also includes an element of faith. This is the irrational component of trust. Trust assumes that the other party will behave in a manner consistent with your interests: If I'm trusting you, it means I trust that you will act in ways that serve me well; this dynamic is what underlies the connection between trust and risk.

The paradox of trust is that it cannot grow unless risks are taken that may result in distrust. Without risk, there is neither need nor utility for trust. Trust and risk give rise to each other. It's rare to discover one without the other. Risk is involved more times than not because we're always making assumptions about how other people are going to behave regarding our interests. In situations where two parties' interests are identical, trust is built in. Trust is facilitated and strengthened by shared understandings of common interests. In the healthiest trusting relationships, the parties regularly acknowledge and attend to their shared interests.

WON AND LOST

Since the Federal Drug Administration was established in 1906, Americans have trusted the drug industry to safely provide prescribed drugs and medicines for a broad variety of ailments and needs. In late September through early October 1982, seven people in the Chicago area died from cyanide poisoning by ingesting Tylenol pills made by Johnson & Johnson. The company's response to that tragedy is still recognized as the gold standard for losing and rebuilding trust with constituents. Johnson & Johnson immediately halted production and advertising for the product, distributed warnings, and recalled all available Tylenol products nationwide. The company also offered to exchange all Tylenol products already purchased by the public. In the immediate aftermath, the company's market share collapsed from 35% to 8%, but it rebounded in less than a year. That success is credited to the company's prompt and aggressive response to the matter. One month after the product tampering, the company reintroduced Tylenol in triple-sealed packages.

Trust can be extended, tempered, or withheld at any time by anyone, and that makes trust a very dynamic motivator that needs constant attention. Trust is something that needs to be built, maintained, and verified, because it can erode quickly. Building back trust after it's been lost is even more daunting.

In sharp contrast to the Tylenol story is the Three Mile Island nuclear accident, which began in Pennsylvania in March 1979. Unlike the quick trust-building response of Johnson & Johnson, the partial meltdown of the Three Mile Island nuclear facility is an example of trust lost and never regained. The reasons for the catastrophe are varied—from mechanical failures and lack of communication to incompetence and ill-equipped machine operators. During the crisis, these inadequacies were compounded by design flaws, including inconveniently arranged instruments and controls.

The 1979 accident crystallized antinuclear safety concerns among activists and the general public and resulted in new regulations for the nuclear industry. It has been cited as a contributor to the decline in the new reactor construction program, a slowdown that was already underway in the early 1970s. The 1979 accident did not initiate the demise of the US nuclear power industry, but it did halt its historic growth.

Trust becomes an issue when others have significant influence over matters that are important to us. The relationship between leaders and constituents pivots substantially on the degree of trust between them. Constituents need their leader's trust to support what they're trying to accomplish, and diminished trust between the two challenges both leaders and constituents to have confidence about what can be expected.

On one hand, trust increases while distrust decreases vulnerability. Everybody is more comfortable exposing their vulnerability in trusting relationships, and displaying vulnerability further increases trust between people. Trust is far easier, less demanding, and offers more possibilities than chronic suspicion.

People trust others when they have shared values. However, sometimes people make assumptions that misperceive, wrongly assess, or ignore alignments and agreements. Parties sometimes don't recognize when understandings and agreements are not shared, and those misalignments can lead to mistakes and problems.

These efforts culminated in the US–Taliban deal in February 2020, which stipulated the withdrawal of all US troops from Afghanistan by 2021. In exchange, the Taliban pledged to prevent any militant group from staging attacks from Afghan territory against the US and its allies. That agreement resulted in the August 30, 2021, final departure of US aircrafts from Afghanistan. One explanation of that abrupt end of the US war in Afghanistan is that the Americans overestimated or didn't pay attention to how much trust the Afghanis had in them. The US assumed the Afghanis trusted the US—that they believed the US had their best interests in mind—but reality seemed to have proven otherwise. The Afghanis cut bait and folded the first opportunity they had, and that was a big miss for the US military. The US military short-changed their responsibility to assess the impact of their actions on trust with the Afghanis.

COMPONENTS OF TRUST

The three components at the foundation of trust are competence, character, and concern. Competence is when you say, "I'm capable." Character is represented by "I'm reliable." Concern is "I care, even if at times it's not in my self-interest."

COMPETENCE

It's hard to trust somebody if they haven't shown they're competent, and trust is always being built in a given context. Setting aside motivation and desire, is this person or organization able to achieve what they say they can? That's what competence is all about, and demonstrating competence builds trust.

Fulfilling obligations and commitments repeatedly and consistently builds trust. What is the track record of a company? Has that team member been able to fulfill their obligations and commitments? Are they willing to bestow their trust in others? Being able to trust others is the first building block of trust.

I worked for a company executive who had an uncanny ability to keep promises and meet deadlines. Like most executives, he carried a cluttered calendar every day. I remember once setting up a meeting for him with a consultant he was considering hiring to do work with one of his sales organizations. The executive had an emergency come up on the day of that meeting, and I really thought he wasn't going to make it. But at the last minute, he showed up and met the consultant as scheduled. One of the enduring memories of that executive is that he always kept his word, and that contributed to the trust that he enjoyed with most members of his organization. He always kept his word. That was a big part of his brand.

CHARACTER

Character, demonstrated by a consistency between what is said and done, is another building block of trust. Character engenders trust. Integrity, an attribute and a perception that can influence understanding and commitment, is a big part of character.

Anthony Fauci is a good example of leadership character. He served as the National Institute of Allergy and Infectious Diseases director from 1984 to 2022. He oversaw an extensive portfolio of basic and applied research to diagnose, prevent, and treat infectious diseases. He served seven presidents and recently gained broad notoriety for his role in leading the United States' response to COVID-19. Throughout his career, his work saved many lives, and although his demonstrated competence is very evident, his character was transcendent in his allegiance to science and its data. He was politically nonpartisan and humble in his demeanor. At the same time, he did and still does have his detractors.

CONCERN

Another word for concern is caring, an attribute that is irrational in the sense that, in caring relationships, people support each other, even in the face of situations that may encourage doing otherwise. Caring is about interests, concerns, positions, and accomplishments as much as it is about people. What you're trying to accomplish is in my self-interest, so I care about you.

Two ways that businesses express caring can be seen in their same-sex partner benefits and maternity- and paternity-leave policies. Regarding same-sex partner benefits, some companies embraced the idea before they had to and implemented benefit policies immediately, while at the other extreme, some companies resisted implementing same-sex benefits policies until they had to under law.

With regard to maternity- and paternity-leave polices, some companies offer maternity leave only for 30–60 days, and other companies offer both maternity and paternity leave for extended periods of time.

BUILDING TRUST

Trust is enabled by intimate familiarity. The kinds of behaviors that build trust are these: openness and honestly disclosing information, along with honesty in words and consistency in action.

Reaching a common understanding about the contextual boundaries of relationships is key to making sure that all parties understand what is and what is not within people's control. It's important to be able to recognize when the other party is disagreeing with or not supporting you and when their actions are a function of rules that supersede choice. Leadership maturity could be at play as well, where the one doing the trusting does or does not understand the limits of what can be expected, due to outside influences.

When you decide whether you can trust someone, you first have to understand whether what you're asking for as a measure of trustworthiness can be provided or whether it simply cannot be demonstrated. It won't work for you to decide not to trust someone if you require them to perform something outside their capabilities.

A high-profile example of this difficulty in expectations played out in the 2020 presidential election when then president Donald Trump argued that the election was rigged and wanted then vice president Mike Pence to overturn the election results and give the election to Trump. Pence refused to do that, claiming he didn't have such authority and that his role in the election vote counting was largely ceremonial. Pence's decision was supported by the rule of law, but Trump lambasted him, portrayed him as a traitor, and drove Trump supporters to chant, "Hang Mike Pence." Trump acted as though his trust had been violated, but he was asking for something beyond Pence's abilities.

The opposite of trust is suspicion. If I don't trust you, that means I'm suspicious of what you may or may not say, mean, or do. Trust is far easier, less demanding, and offers more possibilities than chronic suspicion.

It may seem paradoxical, but to strengthen trust, situations must be created that might blow it all up; the good news is that then, everyone knows the limits of what can and cannot be trusted. And it all ties back to the issue of character; the old joke reminds us that honest politicians won't sell themselves twice.

I had a client once who had a tension-filled relationship with a supplier. The supplier routinely challenged my client's pricing and schedule demands. It seemed to me that my client and this supplier spent an inordinate amount of time negotiating the terms of their agreements. At the same time, my client found that, once the terms were reached and agreed upon, the supplier became a very reliable source, and their relationship flourished.

A TWO-WAY STREET

Trust cuts both ways. It takes two to tango. The things that I need from you for me to trust you I must acknowledge are equivalent to what you need from me to trust me. It's never one-sided. The equivalent of what I need from you, you need from me. What I expect from you, I must be ready to give to you.

And that tees up an important question: Is it more important to be trusting or to be trustworthy? Which is more ennobling? Which is more enlightened? Of course, the answer is both. But if forced to choose, many of my workshop participants feel that being trustworthy is more ennobling and elevated. I believe just the opposite.

It might be counterintuitive, but being trusting is more ennobling because in the absence of being trusting, I deny you the opportunity to prove your trustworthiness. Being trusting is a precondition for your trustworthiness.

Back to the risk again, somebody must go first. Somebody has to say, "Okay, I will invest in you. I will believe in you." Effective leaders always go first. As Hemingway is reputed to have said, "The best way to find out if you can trust somebody is to trust them." If you have a very risk-averse situation, you won't be able to grow the trusting element of the relationship as quickly or as strongly. This is not to suggest that leaders should have blind trust. There is a middle ground. Effective leaders know when and how to give their constituents a chance. Going all the way back to the very root of trust in work relationships, ultimately, the leader and the organization took the first step in trust by hiring you.

Effective leaders demonstrate their trust in the people who report to them by giving them responsibilities to complete important assignments. One client comes to mind who made it very clear whom he trusted and to what degree. He gave some of his direct reports broad customer engagement responsibilities, and to other reports, he gave none. He knew his people's capabilities and knew who he could trust with what kind of work.

The leader must lead with trust. If you want to build trust in the organization, start by trusting people. In my experience, a lot of people go the other way. They want you to prove your trustworthiness, and then they will trust you. And again, that also ties back to the notion of risk. There's much less risk in trusting people who have already demonstrated that they're trustworthy.

PARTNERSHIPS AND COLLABORATIONS

Trust is the foundation upon which high-performance teams and organizations are built. Individual capability and credibility are the bedrock of this trust. A high-performing team or organization has reliable and experienced people. With time and opportunity, individuals can build growing and trusting partnerships that yield even greater achievement.

Trust can be consequential to partnerships and collaborations in several ways. One is trusting that the commitment to achieve is shared and demonstrated. Another is trusting that each team member is accepted and that credit for results is shared appropriately. It is also important to trust that all member opinions and contributions are recognized and valued and that team members will help each other.

Years ago, I had a client who I thought was good at doing that, as he acknowledged team members for their contributions on a regular basis. He held monthly meetings for his large organization and always acknowledged timely contributions made by his team members. He gave appropriate details, so everybody knew who did what and what those efforts yielded. Those recognitions made his team members feel good, and it fortified their loyalty to the organization. That information sharing also served to bring the organization's members closer to each other.

Trusting engagements can include putting one's interests in the hands of another or giving another the use of valuable resources. In all instances, trust is facilitated by a confidence that the other party will do what's in the best interest of all parties to the engagement.

While meaning gains perspective by learning from the past and hope provides energy and excitement to plan for the future, trust gives us confidence to live and engage in the present.

HOW TO CHOOSE TO TRUST

Three important factors should be considered when determining whether to trust someone. First, their history or track record with you provides vital information. Past behavior is the best predictor of future behavior. Second is their character. In addition to assessing how they behaved in the past, the person's character helps you assess their values, how they think and feel, and their alignment with your own values. Even if your relationship is transactional, you must assess the congruence between yourself and the person you are considering trusting. The third consideration is an assessment of their motivations. What do they want out of the arrangement?

In all circumstances, the better you know and understand their performance track record, their values and beliefs, and their motivation for the engagement, the more confident you will be about the decisions you make about the limits of that trust. For engagements that continue over time, attention must be given to guide the relationship forward, whether to sustain, improve, or end it.

Reflection

- Think of people you trust. Why do you trust them? What, if anything, do they have in common with one another?
- Think of a time you trusted someone and they let you down. How did you react? Did it cause you to change your own behavior?
- How do we establish safeguards to ensure that our trust is not abused?

Integrity

The clearer and more precise one can be in their intentions, the easier it is for them to behave with integrity. Working with leaders through the years, I've come to appreciate that leaders like to leave themselves enough room to maneuver, which may mean that they are vague or opaque in their communications. So, like so much else that's been discussed in this book, effective leadership is a balancing act. We don't want too much precision and clarity, which affords no room to maneuver, but we don't want too much vagueness, which can afford too much room to maneuver—allowing the leader to do whatever is expedient.

The practice of being clear and precise is incredibly helpful to someone who wants to act with integrity, while also recognizing that there could be circumstances in which that's not always easy to do. I have a client who I think is exceptional at balancing empowerment and conformity. Generally, she is a very empowering leader. She often gives her constituents clear goals with the latitude of achieving them as they deem best. On the top of her list of exceptions to this practice are circumstances that have the potential of creating risk for the corporation, like matters of product introduction, product allocation, and product phase out. In those situations, strict adherence to company protocols is demanded.

Another example that she offered was in the area of employee development. While this is an ongoing process that takes many forms and should be done often, employee performance appraisals are an annual process that includes specific timelines, meeting protocols, and forms to be completed. For her, the performance appraisal process, as prescribed by the corporation, is precise and invariant.

As a leader, the best way to build trust is to model integrity. Across the entire Heart of the Matter model, integrity is arguably the most impactful leadership characteristic. Just like a rising tide lifts all boats, high integrity lifts all leadership strengths. So, at the end of the day, the most important piece of building leadership effectiveness is modeling integrity, by which I mean proving yourself to be a person of integrity.

While integrity may be a complex concept to explain, it is straightforward to describe behaviorally. Four basic behaviors describe integrity. People with integrity tell the truth as best they know it. They don't make promises they can't keep, or as I learned in Texas, don't make promises with their mouths that their bodies can't cash. They admit their mistakes. And they always do what's best for the larger enterprise.

While that list may be simple to describe, it's not necessarily that simple to execute. How well do you do with these behaviors.? Adhering to these four behaviors consistently and visibly will grow your integrity brand.

Here's a story to illustrate the fourth integrity behavior: always doing what's best for the larger organization. I once had a client who, at the time, was running a large division for a global company. He has since become the CEO of that company. It is common in large organizations that leaders get a higher percentage of their compensation for their unit's performance than for the company's performance.

At the time that I was working with this executive and his team, they were faced with needing to decide whether to do something that would serve the division best in the near term or the larger organization best in the long term. He decided to do what was best for his division in the near term. (I suspect that in his current position as the company's CEO, he would decide differently today.)

I don't think this story illustrates the leader's lack of integrity as much as how integrity takes on different shapes depending upon one's realm of responsibility. In my experience, of these four dimensions, telling the truth as best you know it, not making promises you can't keep, admitting mistakes, and doing what's best for the larger organization, leaders struggle *most* with admitting mistakes. And they can rationalize a lot in order not to admit their mistakes!

I think the broader culture influences that decision pattern.

In organizations that punish people for making mistakes, not admitting them is understandable. In organizations that don't punish people for mistakes, perhaps chalking them up to learning or even applauding people for their honesty and bravery, people will more readily own up to their errors. It's helpful to remember that nobody is more able to influence a culture than the leader. An organization's culture is shaped in large part by what the leader pays attention to.

I once worked with an organization that had a leader who was very dogmatic and blunt with his disappointment over mistakes and poor performance. His people lived and worked in fear of his disapproval. His ways were set in stone and irreversible. When he retired, he was replaced with a new leader who was more people-centric and understanding and who viewed mistakes as teachable moments. As he used to say, "Sometimes, if you can't change the people, you need to change the people." The new leader steadied the ship and brought more stability and less distraction to the journey.

Integrity necessitates an internal moral compass that guides our behavior and decisions. Integrity comes from the word *integrated*, which, when applied to humans, means achieving coherence among daily actions, personal values, and basic aims for accomplishment.

DOING THE RIGHT THING

The 1981 British movie *Chariots of Fire* is a historical sports drama that perfectly illustrates the challenges and triumphs of acting with integrity. The film is based on a true story from the

1924 Olympics in Paris. One storyline involves Eric Liddell, a Scottish sprinter on the UK running team. He was a son of missionaries and a devout Christian, who, upon learning that the qualifying heats for the 100-meter race were scheduled to be run on a Sunday, refused to race because it was the Sabbath.

The sprinter faced intense pressure from the UK authorities to change his mind, including a special meeting with the Prince of Wales, who was also unsuccessful in getting Liddell to change his mind and compete. As Liddell told the Prince of Wales, "I love my country, but my love for God is greater."

The matter was resolved by switching Liddell to run in the 400-meter race, whose qualifying heats were on a Tuesday. Despite many people's expectations that he would falter because of the greater length of that event, Liddell prevailed and won the gold medal.

In the movie, one Olympic committee member remarked that it was a good thing that the committee was unsuccessful in getting Liddell to run in the 100-meter qualifying heats because that would have separated the runner from his beliefs, which were tightly interwoven with his integrity and performance, and he wouldn't have succeeded.

The *Chariots of Fire* story illustrates that separating people from their beliefs and forcing them to do something that they think is wrong doesn't work—if not in the short term, certainly not in the long term.

These considerations underscore the variables and dynamics that can make doing the right thing difficult to determine. For different people, the integrity barrier shifts, and in some circumstances, it's easier to accommodate exceptions. Some people are more flexible than others.

DEVELOPING AND SUSTAINING INTEGRITY

At its core, integrity is the foundation that helps leaders build trust in an organization. The Heart of the Matter suggests that the best way to build trust is to model integrity. Effective leaders understand that to be successful, they need broad support and acceptance from their constituents. They understand that they can't go it alone and that building trust makes it easier for constituents to be supportive. A metaphor from skiing helps illustrate this. Downhill skiers understand that the way to stand up is to lean forward.

Leaders don't have an option to do it any other way. To stay with the skiing metaphor, even if the slope is snowy or icy, leaders still need to lean forward. To do anything else—to lean back or stand upright—will make them fail. Even standing stationary and not moving will make a leader fail, which is the equivalent of managing but certainly not leading. Leading is about freedom, whereas managing is about constraining or worse, coercing. Leadership is not easy. It takes skill and motivation. Both are needed for success.

The notion of trusting and promoting inclusivity and involvement also ties back to a fundamental Heart of the Matter message that the true act of leadership is restoring, promoting, engaging, and enhancing constituents' confidence in their own ability. Give a man a fish, and he eats for a day; teach a man to fish, and he eats for a lifetime.

To say somebody has integrity is to suggest that a person's values, actions, and goals are fully integrated. What they believe, do, and are trying to achieve are intimately connected. Authenticity, although it is often used synonymously with integrity, actually means something else and perhaps more.

I learned the distinction between integrity and authenticity from Robert Terry, who was a professor at the University of Minnesota's Humphrey Institute when I was studying there. He taught me a perspective that distinguishes integrity from authenticity that I find meaningful and helpful.

Authenticity, beyond being true and real to ourselves, is about having a deep understanding of what's true and real in the world. In day-to-day leading, one's actions need to be true for the leader, the situation, and the leader's constituents. Authenticity takes it a step further, suggesting that a leader's "truth" needs to be aligned with a worldview as well. This is a social rather than a personal view of how to engage in work and create processes that enable teams and organizations to build viable and successful futures.

The Heart of the Matter model suggests that leaders provide integrity in service of their constituents' needs for trust, which underscores the leaders' relationships with those constituents. Authenticity takes it a step further and suggests that those relationships also need to be aligned with a larger context.

Reflection

- How can we learn to behave in ways that increase others' trust in us?
- How do we build organizations with the needed trust to compete effectively?
- What decisions or actions can you take to increase trust within your organization?

Reliability and Accountability

Reliability and accountability are not the same thing. Reliability is about performance expectations and assessments, often (if not always) stipulated at or near the outset of a work engagement, and about consistently performing. On the other hand, accountability is more about consequences. It's typically important when violations, errors, mistakes, or mishaps—particularly substantial ones—occur.

From the Nixon resignation and subsequent Ford pardon to the Mueller investigation and subsequent report and testimony, the Epstein horror exposed, as with other high-profile occurrences, new and old, we understand that accountability exercises are about discovering facts, exposing relevant matters, and rendering justice above and beyond punishment.

Ultimately, all well-executed accountability processes are exercises that uncover and discover truth about occurrences and how and where mistakes were made and, as possible, by whom. The last and arguably most difficult accountability process is rendering judgement, because although we have laws, we also have people very vigorously defending positions, even if courts of law don't agree. People in general have differing views about justice and how it's best served.

The way an accountability process is conducted and communicated impacts stakeholder sentiment and even behavior, and that's why they're so important. Understandably, it's easier to hold individuals accountable for transgressions that they've committed than it is to hold leaders accountable for transgressions that their constituents have committed. In 2010, when General Stanley McChrystal and his staff made critical comments about senior administration officials, President Obama dismissed him of his duties.

In contrast, while, through the years, individual Catholic priests have been relieved of their duties (with rare exceptions like the archbishop of Vienna stepping down in 1995 amid sexual abuse allegations), leaders of the Catholic church have generally *not* been punished for the sexual abuse crimes that have plagued the church for many years. The distrust sowed by these unaccountable leaders—and especially their organization's lack of response to it—means a loss of trust between those leaders and their constituents. This is part of why the church is declining: If people don't trust a leader, they won't join their organization. Leaders need to be held accountable for their actions.

The success of an accountability process is largely determined by its visibility and credibility. Because accountability exercises are largely measured by perceptions of how well a matter was addressed, the comprehensiveness of the information examined and the execution of the communications plan for stakeholders is critical. Accountability exercises must be timely as well, because the longer matters take to resolve, the greater the probability they will grow more complicated and difficult to manage.

When organizations are working well, they don't engage in misconduct, nor do they enable it. Their internal mechanisms discover any movements toward misconduct and stop them early. Effective organizations have regulations, compliance guidelines, and inspections. Accountability is woven into the culture.

THE UTILITY OF BEING AN ACCOUNTABLE ORGANIZATION

Being an accountable organization means that units, teams, and individuals all hold themselves accountable for their own work. They are reliable and dependable to execute what's expected of them. That's manifest in the quality of their work and customer interactions. An accountable organization's reputation creates stakeholder admiration, appreciation, and loyalty. Internally accountable organizations enable commitment through effective communication, alignment, and trust.

Individual credibility, integrity, and performance accomplishment are foundational building blocks for all accountable organizations. Two internal mindsets influence that: safety and confidence. Safety is about how secure leaders feel about their position, value, and relationships. Confidence is about a leader's sense of competence and conviction about executing their work effectively. These factors can influence how leaders examine and reflect on their contributions and accountability.

Leaders are challenged to balance being decisive and being circumspect. Overconfidence can cause a person to overlook missed information or mistaken judgements. A leader's tendency to admit or not admit mistakes directly impacts their organization's ability to hold its members accountable when situations require that.

Reflection

- How do you set standards for your group's work output?
- How do you sustain those standards over time?
- How do you foster your constituents' personal accountability?

VALUES CREATE AN INTERNAL COMPASS

Trust and integrity, unlike the other core motivators (meaning and purpose, hope and optimism) necessitate interaction with others, and those interactions are influenced in large part by a leader's integrity, reflected in a mindset that everybody's self-interest is linked and driven by what's in the best interest for the organization. That mindset grows in part from self-reflection, first and foremost about values. Typically, values are stable. They don't change as much as they deepen. As leadership experience grows, values become stronger and more helpful as an internal compass for direction and decisions.

Achieving congruence and alignment with constituents is also an ongoing matter helped by leadership attention. Identifying and assessing relationships for understanding and agreement help leaders navigate forward. Most leaders, with time and attention, can identify which relationships need fortification, support, or appreciation.

Another ongoing leadership exercise on the path to integrity is valuing diversity and unity. Diversity needs unity to be successful. Diversity of experience and perspective can be powerful organizational advantages when enabled and orchestrated effectively. Valuing diversity and developing unity on teams is one way to fortify everybody's sense of reliability and accountability for their work and accomplishments.

Understanding the nature of change and using that to introduce, sustain, and fortify change efforts help leaders influence their constituents. The pandemic started for most of us in 2020 and is an ongoing case study of large-scale change. If nothing else, we're learning how complicated change can be and how difficult it is to influence. Change efforts of any sort are aided by astute leadership attention and integrity.

Leaders build integrity by modeling their values in actions and words. They make themselves visible and familiar to their constituents. They disclose as consistently as possible and use stories to convey perspective and direction. Arguably, integrity is the Heart of the Matter's most powerful leadership effectiveness ingredient.

CHAPTER 8

Support + Growth = Self-Reliance and Leadership Development

Enlightened leaders understand that, to accomplish anything of significance, they need constituents who grow and develop as they work. Accomplishing group purpose is not a static activity, and as circumstances evolve and new and unexpected challenges present themselves, leaders and constituents both need to grow, renew, and adapt to move forward. The most effective leaders build learning and teaching into their own work. In other words, growing and developing people are important responsibilities, arguably a leader's most important responsibilities. Not doing so can impede, derail, or even terminate progress and accomplishment.

The best leaders always have developing others top of mind, and they lead with that. They believe that investing in others creates win–win opportunities for leaders, constituents, and organizations. Different leaders are motivated to do this work for different reasons. For some, it stems from a life value of being helpful. For others, it is a focus on the dividends and rewards for doing this work.

The Heart of the Matter is focused less on why and more on how. Your constituents—those you want to grow and develop—include your direct reports, customers, suppliers, and others with whom you work. In other words, they are people you have the opportunity to influence and help grow.

Leadership is expressed by a combination of behaviors that energize others and encourage people to meet challenging goals. Motivating people to pursue challenging goals is not always easy or pleasant. Sometimes, leaders need to make difficult work demands that can cause discomfort for their constituents. When done right, such situations ultimately yield successful work achievements and develop people's leadership skills at the same time. Effective leaders know how to balance that disequilibrium and keep the work demands and associated stresses in a productive range.

Effective leaders promote and encourage a culture of development. They expand their people's capabilities and consider their next positions and responsibilities. Leaders who grow and develop their people encourage them to take on unfamiliar experiences and think about their careers and suitable next-job opportunities. Influencing and leading is about pushing people into their uncomfortable zones. Sometimes leaders have direct reports who are capable and talented but not good fits for the organization's needs. Good leaders spot those people and situations and move them to responsibilities that are better fits, even if that means losing talent.

Effective leaders know their people, and they know what their people want, and in a perfect world, they can slot them into positions that provide both what those people want and what the organization needs. That's why it's so important that leaders know their constituents—their capabilities, interests, and motivations. Effective leaders know what their employees aspire to and discover ways to help them achieve those aspirations, even if that means encouraging them to leave the organization for better-suited opportunities.

I once had a client who was masterful at appointing people throughout his organization to assignments that benefited the individuals involved and the overall organization as well. I remember him orchestrating one particular set of tricky circumstances. My client's organization had four general managers who, in turn, each had an average of four directors, who each, in turn, were directly responsible for the work of several individuals. In this story, it was a time when one of my client's directors left the organization for another opportunity. Consensus identified person X for the position, but to the surprise of many, a different person was chosen. Shortly thereafter, person X was lateralled to a position in another organization, and less than a year later, the same person X was promoted to a vice president position to run a separate business within the division. I am not certain about how many of the steps in these moves were orchestrated by my client or others, but it wasn't happenstance or coincidence. It was the result of thinking and adhering to the long game. My client was playing chess, not checkers. Good leaders do that.

Leadership and Authority

When guiding people through change, leaders use authority and influence. These two traits are different, although they often coexist. The leader's challenge, as always, is to balance them: They must know how and when to demand (to use their authority) and when to influence.

Leaders decide when and how to influence and direct their people. It's always easier to decide which approach to take when the problems being addressed have reliable solutions to be implemented. In those situations, leading with authority is best.

Authority figures fix things. They deliver solutions from without. Authority figures respond to their constituents' needs for resources, direction, protection, and role clarification. They tell their constituents what to do.

I had a client once who was a fixer. He cleaned up organization and business messes. His relationship with the organization leader was deep and had been in place for many years. They knew and trusted each other. He was often called upon to clean up problems, terminate contracts, and replace employees as needed. He was very good at what he did, but his overall leadership effectiveness suffered for it. He was often impatient and short with people. Yet there was no doubt he did one thing really well: He knew how to clean up messes and get—and keep—the company out of trouble. The leader realized this and helped the fixer focus on fixing. People play different roles in any organization, and when circumstances permit, the organization's needs must align with the skills and interests of the most available individual.

A LEADER'S NEW DIRECTION MIGHT MEAN KICKING OLD HABITS

When the best directions are not obvious, a leader provides solutions that people need to grow into. In those situations, personal discipline is needed to focus on what needs to be learned to move forward. Sometimes that means helping people change lifelong habits. This is very difficult work, and often these types of situations necessitate changes that come from within.

Many years ago, I was a cigarette smoker. Then, as now, there was a lot of compelling evidence for why to quit, but for an extended period, I was unable to stop smoking. Mark Twain said, "Quitting is easy; I've done it many times." That was me. I smoked, then stopped for six months, then I started again, until the next time, when I stopped for whatever period and then started again. This cycle of smoking, stopping, and then starting again went on for about two years. I finally stopped smoking for good when I developed a mindset change to stop viewing myself as a smoker trying to quit and started viewing myself as a nonsmoker.

Changing the habits of a lifetime often requires transformation, becoming somebody different or new. My personal example of becoming a nonsmoker was a combined effort of my internal commitment to being a nonsmoker and others' encouragement and support to do so. In a work context, transformational work is aided by efforts that leaders make. Arguably, successful change efforts necessitate both, but growth comes from adaptive work more than by problem solving.

Reflection

- Think of a time you needed to overcome a bad habit. Were you successful?
- What led to your success or your failure?
- Have you ever tried to see yourself in a different light, the way I did in order to quit smoking? (If not, try it!)
- Have you tried to help others overcome habits that weren't serving them well? How did that work out, and what methods seemed most helpful? Least helpful?

Adaptive Work

Adaptive work is needed when technical solutions are not working or insufficient. It's important to distinguish technical solutions from adaptive work. The two offer very different ways of framing issues. Arguably, they both have utility, but encouraging adaptive work is often much more challenging than seeking, discovering, and implementing technical solutions. Adaptive work always challenges people to break long-held habits. It provides much greater challenges at the outset but often offers more enduring solutions.

For example, most growing cities have traffic issues. That certainly has been an issue in Austin, Texas, where I live. The solution offered and, in many cases, implemented was roadway expansion. Lanes were expanded and added to congested arteries. These are technical solutions. Another solution is to educate, encourage, and incentivize people to accept and embrace completely different approaches to addressing an issue. That might mean expanding public transportation, creating pedestrian- and bike-friendly infrastructure, and creating mixed-use developments to bring where we live, work, and shop closer together. These solutions look beyond the technical, but they are harder to implement immediately and may be more costly in the short term. Arguably, the trade-off is that what takes longer to implement endures and withstands change more effectively.

I remember going to a forum that was convened specifically to address the traffic issue. One speaker offered that, even if these technical solutions could be implemented quickly, traffic congestion problems would still exist. Alternatively, he offered solutions that encouraged people to change their driving habits and patterns. Those solutions, using public transportation, carpooling, and the like, necessitate people to change the habits of a lifetime. Created years ago, carpool lanes restricted vehicles from using certain roadways unless those vehicles were occupied by multiple passengers. This is a good example of the difference between providing technical solutions and encouraging adaptive behavior.

Generally, technical solutions are easier to develop and implement but are seldom as durable. Even though carpooling is less expensive and eases parking problems, many drivers prefer—by habit, by choice, or both—to drive alone to and from work. Effective leaders motivate their constituents to make short-term sacrifices for more appealing long-term gains, but that's not easy.

SEAT BELTS AND CIGARETTES

Two examples of successful adaptive work involve cars and cigarettes. One promoted wearing seat belts while driving or riding in cars, and the other promoted restricting opportunities to smoke cigarettes outside the home. Both have law enactment and robust education and advertising to help people change habits of a lifetime. Today, many more people wear seat belts while driving, and fewer people smoke cigarettes.

Regarding seat belt use, it took decades before wearing a seat belt became common practice. The concept was introduced by Volvo in 1959. In 1961, Wisconsin became the first state to require seat belts to be installed in all vehicles. In 1973, an interlocking system was installed in cars that would not permit them to start before seat belts were secured. However, the public reacted very unfavorably to that, and the interlocking system requirement was removed. In 1983, a seat belt case reached the Supreme Court, and on the strength of another party of interest—the insurance industry—the Supreme Court reinstated the requirement to install seat belts in all vehicles. In 1984, New York became the first state to require seat belt use, and all states have followed suit since then, with the exception of New Hampshire.

The evolution of seat belt use in the United States went from requiring cars to have them installed to requiring people to wear them. Today, "buckle up" signs are common on streets and roadways to remind drivers and passengers what to do.

The country's evolution from smoking to nonsmoking was a bit more challenging, although it followed a similar evolutionary path. There were two powerful features of that situation, one internal and one external, that were working against that change.

Nicotine is addictive, which is more challenging than simply replacing old habits with new ones. Also, the tobacco industry is a powerful lobby whose self-interest, making money, is a strong motivator. Yet not unlike seat belts, time and multipronged approaches finally drove change. A TV segment on *60 Minutes* back in 1993 exposed the widespread effort by the tobacco industry to debunk the truly addictive nature of tobacco, and the multiple harms it causes. Arguably, that exposé did irreparable harm to the tobacco industry. Just like with seat belts, a multipronged approach of research, advertising, and rules restricting where people can smoke has caused a downward trend in tobacco consumption.

Wholesale change in companies with rigid and well-defined hierarchies can happen more quickly. I once worked in a company that had traditional conservative dress codes for all employees. It wasn't written down anywhere, but people knew them. Everybody understood that meetings with executives required the men to wear suit jackets in addition to ties, which were omnipresent.

At one point, the company hired a new CEO who had not grown up in the company. His previous employer operated with a more relaxed dress code. This man never wore ties, and his shirts were open at the neck. Once people understood that the new leader didn't have the same dress code requirements as his predecessor did, in a very short period, most male employees stopped wearing ties. It was a classic example of modeling. People pay attention to what executives do and say and often copy those behaviors.

THE FUTURE OF ADAPTIVE WORK

The world of work, broadly, is facing a sea change, and as of this writing in 2023, the final chapter has yet to be written. The pandemic of 2020 forced many to work from home, and as the severity of the pandemic subsides, getting people to return to work has been challenging. One side of the argument says that working from home creates better balance and less stress, and, as a result, it leads to no productivity loss and maybe even results in productivity gains. The other side argues that having employees come to work increases productivity and strengthens organizational culture. Some companies are mandating that employees return to work, if not full time, at least part time. Other companies are incentivizing employees to return to work with team-building activities and celebrations. Ultimately, like with the seat belts and smoking change processes, time will tell how this evolves.

Leadership comes from within, although sometimes somebody instigates and inspires new perspectives to consider. The classic example that endures is President Kennedy's moon speech. That speech inspired the entire nation. Beyond the success of the first moon landing on July 20, 1969, the achievement inspired many to start thinking about things in different ways, in ways that are not incremental, in ways that force people to make changes and not just react or implement technical solutions.

Several technological innovations are attributable to the learnings gathered from the success of the Apollo moon landings. One was the advancement in breathing systems used by firefighters. Although NASA did not invent them, NASA was responsible for making them usable by making them light and efficient. The improved system was lighter and easier to wear, and the face masks allowed for a wider field of view. NASA also collaborated with Martin Marietta Company to develop tools to help astronauts collect moon rock samples. The custom-designed cordless rotary hammer drill was one invention that has since seen broad application on Earth. Moonboot material has revolutionized athletic footwear, improving shock absorption and providing superior stability and motion control. Houston's NRG Stadium features the first retractable roof of its kind, made possible by NASA technology as well. NASA's space suit fabric has fostered many new innovations too.

Taking on adaptive work becomes more pressing when technical solutions are not adequate. Something more needs to be done. It takes bringing together differences and fostering conflict in service of learning. That is tricky because things could get out of hand. Adaptive work acknowledges that it creates disequilibrium, stress, and difficult adjustments.

Transformational Leadership

Transformational leaders mobilize adaptive work while developing leadership skills in others. They act with integrity. They make it easy for people to trust them. Transformational leaders have compelling views about the future and what their organizations can do to grow and influence direction. Some have five-year plans or even more. Most organizations look out at least 18 months and develop plans that identify and enable growth.

Adaptive work can be difficult and disruptive. It often demands changing habitual behaviors and practices. Influence and support are the most important tools leaders have and use to instigate adaptive work. Transformational leaders bring together people with disparate views about goals or methods and spark conflicts that, when used effectively, initiate learning that helps reframe what needs to be done. This work creates disequilibrium by throwing the status quo out of balance—and transformational leaders know how to keep this disequilibrium in the productive range.

Transformational leaders foster enthusiasm, intensity, and resilience. They motivate their constituents by broadening their aspirations, goals, and values. They understand that they're always being observed and that their actions, what they say and do, and how they interact and engage with colleagues and constituents, influence and motivate constituent behavior to develop and exercise discipline and break entrenched habits. They stimulate their constituents intellectually by discussing and challenging assumptions about important matters. Team meetings are excellent forums for that work.

Transformational leaders develop constituent skills and encourage confidence to perform beyond expectation. Role modeling is the best way to develop constituents for adaptive work. Transformational leaders display the way they work. Their accomplishments are known or can be discovered easily. They do their work and develop people at the same time. They also promote healthy relationships with everybody. They always look for shared objectives, try to understand people's motivations, and learn how best to build on them.

Coaching and mentoring go hand in hand with role modeling as effective tools for building constituent success. Effective coaching and mentoring take time to build healthy, trusting relationships. Transformational leaders don't miss opportunities for their constituents to be exposed to and engaged in adaptive work—this is, changing habits and creating discipline.

Throughout history, there have been many transformational leaders, and for me, the person at the top of that list is Mahatma Gandhi, for the way he employed nonviolent resistance to lead the successful campaign for India's independence from British rule and later inspired movements for civil rights and freedom across the world.

Another transformational leader, certainly not on the order of Gandhi but nonetheless a transformational leader, was John Wooden, who coached the UCLA men's basketball team from 1948 to 1975. His teams' successes through the years were like none achieved before or since. It was his successes beyond coaching that made him transformational. He was revered by all and much beloved by his former all-star players, among them Lew Alcindor (later Kareem Abdul-Jabbar) and Bill Walton. Wooden was renowned for his short, simple inspirational messages to his players, which were directed at how to be a success in life as well as in basketball.

In one of his first coaching sessions, he spent time teaching players how to lace their shoes. It was also Wooden's style to intervene very infrequently during games. He lived the philosophy that his work was done in practice and that his players' work was done in games. His leadership legacy transcends sports with impact and influence in the worlds of business, personal success, and organizational leadership.

Reflection

- How do you broaden your constituents' perspective?
- How do you build their confidence?
- How well do you coach your constituents?
- Have you seen any transformation in them, or in yourself, as a result of your coaching?

The perfect example of transformation is the caterpillar turning into a butterfly—simply becoming something completely new and different. Humans can't do that, but they can make changes to their behavior, even habituated ones. Transformational leaders mobilize adaptive work and keep their constituents' disequilibrium in a productive range. They're influenced by their values and driven by their commitment to a purpose and mission for their organization. Selfish or myopic motivations do not serve transformational leaders. Demanding work can be difficult to manage and necessitates knowing people well to predict how they each would react to certain challenges and how well they'd embrace and undertake them.

Against the daunting challenge of changing lifetime habits and doing things that don't feel comfortable in the near term, effective leaders focus on their people, the future, and how the organization can influence them by using broader goals, wider aspirations, and organizational values. Transformational leaders sustain a strong culture that is manifested in consistent behavior and practices that help everybody understand what should be expected from them. Environments in which shared values are well established, supported, and practiced help leaders influence people to look beyond their self-interest to greater interests for the group.

CUSTOMER SATISFACTION

Transformational leaders influence customer-centric organizations. The belief is that adding value to customers is a strong motivational force. Getting excited about delivering value to customers, meeting their needs, is a second-to-none motivation. Effective leaders connect their constituents with their customers and help them understand customer needs and the organization's role in meeting them.

One story comes from work I once did with an IT organization. The issue at the time was spam; a lot of spam and junk mail was coming through. In response, the IT organization implemented programs that successfully filtered much of that out. One of their customers, also a client of mine, noticed the marked improvement in the state of his inbox and sent a complimentary note to the head of the IT department. He told me that story, and neither of us had any idea about the impact that note had on the organization.

Sometime later, I was conducting a workshop with these same IT people on feedback and told them the story of my other client's note to the head of their IT department. To a person, they all said, "We know that story." I was surprised that my other client's thank-you note was so renowned. They explained that the department head sent that note around to everybody, because they rarely got any sort of positive feedback, although they often received complaint notes. They were often told what they did wrong but were rarely told what they did right. My client had thanked them for doing something right, and it inspired them. Giving constituents and clients alike appropriate positive feedback can serve as a very powerful motivator.

This story underscores an important leadership question about how well constituents know what their customers think about their work and how the leader uses that information to the team's benefit. Effective leaders understand that work meaning resides in customer satisfaction, so it's incumbent that leaders understand who their customers are and what they expect and appreciate.

Reflection

- Do you spend sufficient time studying and understanding what your customers value about your organization's work?
- Do you share and discuss that shared understanding among your constituents?

UNDERSTANDING THE VALUE OF YOUR WORK

An organization I worked with for a while at one point came to the realization that their technical community, the people who designed and formulated their products, had never visited customers. Once they realized that, they built customer visits into the laboratory's routines. The technical teams started meeting their customers throughout the design process: at the outset of projects to better understand the needs that their products were to address, in the middle of projects to monitor performance and make adjustments as necessary, and once the projects were completed to assess their products' overall performance and success.

Another client once told me that he would periodically leave his desk and take walks to the loading dock and watch the employees load trucks to be reminded about what it is that they really did. The effective leader, the transformational leader, helps their constituents understand the importance of their work.

Transformational leaders help their constituents understand higher aspirations and goals. They also value and support developing their constituents' skills and confidence to perform beyond expectation. One way to do that is role modeling. Effective leaders don't ask their constituents to do things they don't do. Effective leaders encourage their constituents to question assumptions and the status quo while also remaining mindful of the tension this can create, because questioning can slow things down. Arguably, transformational leaders spend most of their time mentoring and coaching.

It's really important that transformational leaders convey their confidence to their constituents that those constituents can make difficult adaptations and take on challenging journeys and come through them successfully. I had a client who, at his monthly meetings, routinely reported about different teams' progress, challenges, and successes. One could feel the pride he took with his teams' work and the confidence he had in them to succeed.

Transformational leaders resist the temptation of always assigning work to people who do it really well—missing opportunities to stretch and grow them in other areas—and give work to people who do things they don't necessarily do well to work on projects that might be a bit away from what they usually do in service of broadening them, connecting them with other people from whom they can learn new information and processes. From my experience, putting people in new stretch assignments embedded with a team increases the return on that investment substantially.

There's been a fair amount of research done by Gallup that suggests focusing on people's strengths proves to be more useful than fixing their deficiencies.[11] Transformational leaders lead their constituents' existing strengths to new opportunities. The trick is to provide work that fortifies and stretches their strengths, not just reuses them. The challenge for the leader is to place people in situations that benefit from their strengths while also growing and broadening them.

Reflection

1. How well do you know your constituents' strengths and interests?
2. How do you leverage those understandings for your constituents', your own, and others' growth and development?

---

11 Marcus Buckingham and Donald Clifton, *Now, Discover Your Strengths* (The Free Press, 2001).

Remember what my client used to say: "If you can't change the people, you need to change the people." Sometimes, changes make people into something they weren't, and other times people need to be switched out for a better fit elsewhere.

I knew a guy who spent his entire career with a package delivery company and retired from the company having had a successful career as an HR executive. I remember him telling me that, at one point, he was being sent out of town to learn how to drive the company's big trucks. The culture of that organization was such that, regardless of one's responsibilities and career path, having that experience of being behind the wheel of a big truck, understanding the difficulty and challenges of the job, made them better at whatever it was that they eventually did for the company. It was also a common bond among the employees. That experience created a shared experience among all employees, regardless of work discipline, function, or level. It exposed them to their common purpose.

Effective leaders are conscious and consistent in their words, actions, and gestures, because constituents interpret these and use them to make sense of situations. Not a perfect example, but I remember a company manufacturing director telling me a story about a plant visit he made. At one point, as he passed by a piece of equipment, he asked how long it had been sitting there. They answered him, and the next day, when they passed the same location, that piece of equipment was gone. When he asked where that piece of equipment had gone, they said, "You told us to move it." Sometimes, constituents attribute meaning and interpret what their leaders say even when the leader doesn't say it. Sometimes tone is more important than words because it can convey meaning and understanding without intention, because what is said can lend itself to interpretation.

Transformational leadership is difficult. Sometimes it demands adherence to discipline, which could force the leader out of their comfort zone. Being able to communicate consistently and calmly isn't always easy to do.

Leadership Illustrated

There is a particular scene in the movie *Saving Private Ryan* that illustrates transformational leadership in an instant, an exchange between Captain Miller (Tom Hanks) and Private Reiben (Edward Burns). The unit had just survived an enemy attack in which they lost two men. They also captured a prisoner of war.

Captain Miller, knowing that they couldn't take the prisoner with them, had the prisoner blindfolded and instructed him to walk 100 paces in a particular direction in hopes that an Allied troop would find and secure him. One soldier, Private Reiben, took great exception to this decision and expressed as much, refusing to accept Miller's order to fall in. At that point, Sergeant Horvath (Tom Sizemore) intervened and pulled his gun on Reiben, creating a standoff between the two.

The other soldiers saw what was going on and started screaming at Captain Miller to do something. Miller let the confrontation escalate until right before the breaking point and then explained that he had been a schoolteacher in Pennsylvania, something none of the troops knew until that point but had been interested in learning about. That quieted the shouting, and everybody paused. Miller went on to explain that all he wanted to do was get home to his wife, and if finding Private Ryan would make that happen, then those were his orders to follow. He then told Private Reiben that if he wanted to go and fight the war rather than stay with this unit and continue searching for Private Ryan, Miller would not object and would even process the paperwork to make that happen. Reiben took all that in and, after a long moment of reflection, fell in with the rest of the troops.

Captain Miller understood early on that his order, to find and save one soldier, was not like conventional assignments of war, to find and defeat the enemy. When tensions reached a boiling point and two of his soldiers were fighting with each other, one threatening to kill the other, Captain Miller understood that he needed to shift everybody's focus from determining how to deal with a prisoner of war to the mission's larger purpose of finding a way to get home—a purpose that everybody shared. He also never forced Private Reiben to do anything and ultimately gave him the choice.

Transformational leaders help their constituents discover meaning in their work and the motivation to accomplish it.

Impactful Leadership

Leading adaptive work requires listening to people's ideas and concerns both inside and outside the organization to help determine whether technical solutions or adaptive work is needed. Often, leaders are confronted with both, which challenges them to determine how to spend their time, energy, and resources. Effective leaders move toward better balance in prioritizing what to do when.

Transformational leaders pay attention to and surface conflicts in order to help shape needed changes. This also helps assess their people's values, attitudes, and behaviors and identify those that need to change to make progress. These leaders also keep everybody focused on the real issues rather than on blaming others, on external forces, or on workloads. Rather, they communicate about the group's challenges and invite constituent debate to help clarify assumptions behind competing perspectives and values.

Effective leaders suppress the instinct to provide solutions and grow accountability among constituents. They help their groups take the initiative and then encourage them to define and solve problems. In general, they are more supportive than controlling.

Effective leaders expose conflict by asking key questions, and they protect people who speak out. They also value curiosity more than obedience. They also regulate disequilibrium and keep things productively balanced by managing the rate of change and the sequence and pace of work, and by prioritizing new initiatives. They also stop the ongoing low-value projects to make room for new ones.

Transformational leaders communicate confidence and have the emotional capacity to tolerate uncertainty, frustration, and pain. It takes a special kind of person to be a transformational leader. It is difficult work. It demands intellectual and physical capacity, and much more.

Effective leaders do a better job at balancing the long and the short view. It's always a matter of trade-offs—fixing something and creating something else in the process versus deciding to just live with it. Time is a variable that impacts everything.

When the focus of the Heart of the Matter model moves from the primary dimensions (purpose–meaning, optimism–hope, integrity–trust) to the supporting dimension (growth–support), it offers a deeper level of change: transformational change in service of building something that can perpetuate itself over time. Those are not technical solutions. Technical solutions are easier to implement and offer near-term dividends that may or may not endure.

The Heart of the Matter, on the other hand, offers opportunities to develop and share perspectives that align people and organizations around shared, purpose-driven work, in open and supportive environments.

CHAPTER 9

The Heart of the Matter Model in Balance

Like all matters about leadership effectiveness, it's all a matter of balance. Like I said earlier, the Goldilocks moment is when things are not too hard and not too soft, when things are not too hot and not too cold, but just right. Effective leaders are always asking three questions: What does balance look and feel like? Where is our balance now? And how do we need to move or change to achieve greater balance? They also work on developing and implementing tools and methods that help improve individual, team, and organization balance. The Heart of the Matter is a model that explains primarily social and interpersonal phenomena between leaders and their constituents rooted in understandings about human motivation and performance.

The utility of the Heart of the Matter model is that it helps explain relationships between leaders and those they influence. The Heart of the Matter model focuses on motivation as the catalyst for all that needs to get done. Earlier in the book, the core motivation pairs, purpose–meaning, optimism–hope, and integrity–trust, are described in a cause-and-effect manner that drives interactions between leaders and constituents. The model is flexible, not rigid, and allows for differences across leaders, constituents, and circumstances. At the same time, the model identifies those core motivation pairs, purpose–meaning, optimism–hope, and integrity–trust, that are relevant to everybody.

Earlier in the book, the Heart of the Matter was explained as a linear cause-and-effect model with three primary motivators—purpose, optimism, and integrity—that focus and drive interactions between leaders and constituents. It explains the model's foundations.

The next step in understanding the model's potential utility is to examine the interactions among its core motivators—purpose–meaning, optimism–hope, and integrity–trust—to explain how the core motivators work together (See Figure 9.1). This view of the Heart of the Matter's core motivators helps build approaches for developing and supporting other leaders.

INTERACTIONS AMONG THE CORE MOTIVATORS

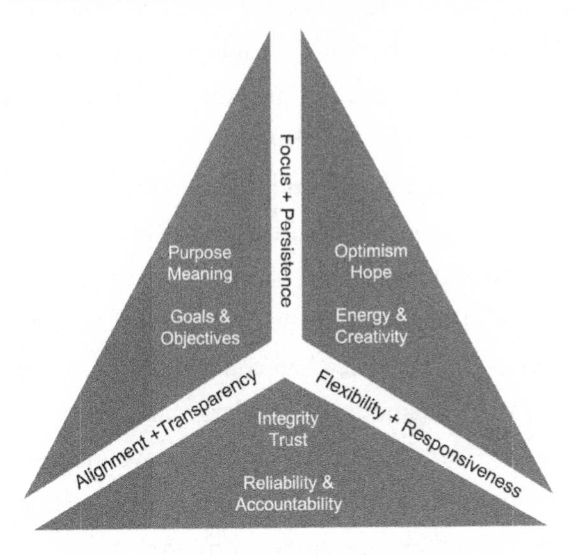

Figure 9.1

The triangular depiction in Figure 9.1 focuses on the Heart of the Matter's core motivator sets and how they interact to help achieve greater balance and effectiveness. The Heart of the Matter model viewed this way offers additional ideas and suggestions for building and assessing greater balance.

This depiction of the motivator pairs focuses on how they interact and contribute to leadership and organization effectiveness. There are three interfaces in the triangle approach. The first is between purpose–meaning and optimism–hope. The second interface is between optimism–hope and integrity–trust, and the third interface is between integrity–trust and purpose–meaning. Viewed together, all three interface descriptions provide suggestions and guidance for assessing and developing organization balance and leadership effectiveness.

Because the triangle and matrix visualizations of the Heart of the Matter model have identical ingredients, the same relationships between the core motivators remain; none have priority or importance over the others. Also, in both depictions, the ingredients are fluid and interact with all of the other model components. Remember, the Heart of the Matter is more art than science.

The key to utilizing both ways of visualizing the model is seeing trends. Effective leaders constantly make assessments of organization balance and regularly take stabs at figuring out who needs to do what when to achieve greater balance. The precision of these assessments is not as important as simply attending to them and noticing trends.

All three of the triangle interfaces are labeled to focus, in turn, on the quality and strength of each interface's condition. Reviewing the quality and strength of targets and tendencies that describe a leader or organization helps identify and influence balance.

Focus and Persistence

Figure 9.1 identifies focus and persistence at the interface between purpose–meaning and optimism–hope. Idealized individuals and organizations with strong balance at this interface are very clear about what they aim to achieve. They do not get distracted easily from work priorities and demands. They follow through on planning, remain appropriately patient, and exhibit admirable resilience.

Unlike persistence, which is primarily an internal ability, focus is more prone to be influenced by others: supervisors, customers, and anybody else who has access to you. That makes setting and executing priorities potentially more challenging. And then there's change itself. Therefore, it's very important to understand your focus, your rationale for it, and what's changing.

Persistence is a conversation between your interest and your energy. Persistence is at the heart of your motivation. Much of what influences motivation is internal drive wired by something in your brain that says *IT'S IMPORTANT!* And you stay with it as long as it's important.

Reflection

- Does your schedule allow the time needed to attend to important matters?
- How distracted from big projects do you get for smaller, easier, and less significant projects and work?
- Is it your nature to work on reports, presentations, etc. more than you should?
- What other important questions or reflections should you be considering?

Flexibility and Responsiveness

Flexibility and responsiveness sit at the interface between optimism–hope and integrity–trust. Individuals and organizations with strong balance at this interface are not rigid; they understand what can and cannot be done, and they're energetic and highly communicative, especially with work collaborators.

Flexible and responsive leaders and organizations have pace. They're not prone to overthinking or overanalyzing matters. They're not rash, simply confident with their data, thoughts, and ideas. Leaders of flexible and responsive organizations invest in their people and let them know how important their contributions are. They encourage and reward confidence.

Reflection

- How important is customer responsiveness in your organization, and how do you know that?
- How easy or difficult is it for you and your team to attend to disruption and to change direction?
- What are your particularly rigid and alternatively flexible practices? If they're not how they should be, how can you improve that?
- What other important questions or reflections should you be considering?

Alignment and Transparency

The third interface, described as alignment and transparency, lives at the interface of purpose–meaning and integrity–trust. This interface is affected by the clarity of desired outcomes and the confidence people have about their colleagues (their capability and commitment), especially those whose work is integral to the success of their own.

In my experience, alignment issues have their root cause in communication. For many reasons, not the least of which is work pace and complexity, keeping people and groups of people informed and aligned takes attention and effort. An organization, a team, or a leader is aligned when they understand how their work connects with others'. Is it a customer–client relationship? Is it as collaborators? Effective leaders make, facilitate, and nurture those connections.

Transparency has its root in trust. Transparency reflects trust, typically within an organization. As I discussed earlier when explaining integrity, four behaviors underpin trust and trust building. Tell the truth as best you know it. Keep your promises. Admit mistakes. Always do what's best for the enterprise. Those are not always easy to do, but deliberate effort and consistency in practice will strengthen the trust between yourself and others.

Reflection

- How thoroughly and quickly does information travel through the organization?

continued

- In general, do people who need to know learn new information in a timely manner?
- Are your organization's communications systems adequate for your needs?
- What other important questions or reflections should you be considering?

This model can help leaders and organizations assess balance and help guide where attention is needed. Effective leaders, always in search of better balance, continually review this report card—focus and persistence, flexibility and responsiveness, and alignment and transparency—for where and how they, their leadership teams, and the organization can discover ways to achieve better balance.

With this view and understanding of the Heart of the Matter leadership effectiveness model, we now have a composite report card on balance. Balanced leaders and organizations are focused and persistent, flexible and responsive, and aligned and transparent. Assess yourself, your team, your organization. Have those assessments take the form of conversation. It's less important what tool you use and much more important to have open, fair, and candid conversations about the behavior patterns observed, their meaning, and what steps will lead to improvement.

Near the end of my workshops, I often ask participants to apply a test of sufficiency to the Heart of the Matter model:

What about leadership does the model not account for? One participant once commented that the Heart of the Matter doesn't acknowledge the importance of promoting fun in the workplace.

I distinguish between fun and play in the workplace. For me, play is happy hour, birthday celebrations, off sites, and the like. Such activities, appropriately framed and facilitated, can add immense value to your workplace's balance between play and work. In general, the Heart of the Matter indeed does not speak to workforce play. On the other hand, fun to me is about being engaged in meaningful work with confidence that the work's objectives can be achieved while working with trustworthy people who share common purpose. In other words, for me, the Heart of the Matter is all about fun.

Conclusion

"The process of becoming a leader is much the same as the process of becoming an integrated human being."

—WARREN BENNIS

Nothing underscores that effective leadership is an art more than the reality that there is no single formula for effective leadership. Effective leadership meets context and constituents and crafts a way to move forward and make progress. This approach is set in a mindset that it's not about knowing or doing everything right as much as it is a matter of always moving forward and getting better.

The process of becoming and being an effective leader is not easy. Growing and developing leaders, which means helping others become more skillful and artful in the ways they interact with and influence other people, is a formidable undertaking and requires principled commitment and dedication to push forward where setbacks could be common. Furthermore, the act of developing leaders is an act of leadership development. Growing other leaders grows leadership. Whether focused on one's own leadership development or that of others or entire organizations, developing leaders means helping them align their values, their aims for accomplishment, and their behavior, so that those elements are attached to a larger purpose. As has been mentioned before, that means habituating on four practices: telling the truth, keeping promises, admitting mistakes, and working in the best interest of the larger organization, most if not all of the time.

The challenges and requirements for being an effective leader are many. Growing one's own leadership effectiveness and developing others' skills can be challenging and should not be entertained lightly. Whether you're trying to improve yourself or others, the time and effort must be thoughtful and thought through. Prerequisite to that, effective leaders are principled. Principles are what matter and are important. Principles are unshakable truths that are held dear and very rarely if ever violated for any reason. Typically, people form them early and strengthen them over time, and they influence how to interact with others.

Effective leaders carve out time for restoration. Absent some means for restoration, burnout is eventual and inevitable.

Reflection

- What are the surefire ways you recognize when you're on tilt?
- What do you do if you find yourself there?
- What do you do on a regular basis to help keep yourself in balance?
- Who are your go-to people—those who listen and offer advice when you ask for it?
- What other important questions or reflections should you be considering?

The next needed ingredient for leadership effectiveness is purpose. Purpose is always larger than any one person, which means that achieving purpose requires the involvement and support of others. Effective leaders are not selfish. They are driven by a commitment to purpose and constituents. As needed, leaders protect their constituents but primarily grow and develop them.

Effective leaders are always balancing tensions between demands, often in opposition to each other, on spectra such as short term–long term, fast (impulsive)–slow (reflective), diplomacy–restraint, curiosity–judgement, and ideas–emotions. These demands and others are primarily fluid, not static.

Success and managing tensions demand attention, principled flexibility, and discipline. It's like spinning plates.

These are tall orders, and the most effective leaders understand that leadership development is always a work in progress. All of us are flawed, so we should all know better than to strive to be perfect or help others be perfect. Simply strive to get better.

An activity that I use at the end of my workshops is to ask attendees to write themselves a letter about their leadership effectiveness and how to improve it. Having read this book, I think you can do that right now yourself. Reflect on what you've learned, thought, and felt while reading this book, and then write yourself a brief letter about the aspects of your leadership that you want to improve. Don't carve out too much—just something you think you can and want to make better. Set that letter aside for 30 days and then mail it to yourself.

My workshop participants have told me that when they get that letter in the mail, it helps them measure the progress they've already made and the further progress they need to commit to. Try this exercise, please, and I hope it helps you sustain your commitment to improving your own leadership effectiveness.

Acknowledgments

This work would not have been possible without all the opportunities that many leaders gave me to learn from and support them. The task of identifying all the people who taught me, whom I learned from, and whom I consulted with is too daunting for me. Those people span my entire career. I am not going to mention any by name because there are many. And I don't want to add the risk of leaving somebody out who should have been mentioned. Maybe it's a cop-out, but my wish is that former clients see themselves in my stories. For everybody else, may you find the perspectives and suggestions helpful.

That said, there is one person I would like to acknowledge: Paul Woodruff, who passed away in September 2023. He was a University of Texas professor who was paired with me by the Human Dimensions of Organizations (HDO) leaders to teach our workshop, the Heart of Leadership. Paul helped me in so many ways. He helped me understand how best to convey the workshops' messages. Words can't describe his brilliance and impact on me as an educator, consultant, and practitioner.

complexity of the company, as well as its age and history, consistently offered interesting and challenging work. While he was there, AJ worked with leaders experienced in different specialties, work objectives, and structures. Across all those people and their leadership stories, a common thread was intellect and honesty. Most people AJ worked with were smart and honest. Generally, that was a very pleasant culture to work in.

In 2015, AJ retired from the company but not from his profession. He now spends his professional time teaching and consulting. The transition has been wonderful. He enjoys a host of clients, varied in their work directions and challenges but all united in a quest for better leadership. Writing this book seemed like the right thing to do next. Of course, AJ plans to continue teaching and consulting. You can contact AJ at aj@ajjosefowitz.com.

About the Author

Photo by Camille J Wheeler

AJ JOSEFOWITZ is a leadership development consultant, coach, and trainer who resides in Austin, Texas. While completing his PhD work at the University of Minnesota, AJ held an internship with a newly forming corporate human resources development organization at Honeywell. That was a beneficial and instructive career-impacting experience. He subsequently worked for Honeywell Bull, a partnership between Honeywell and CII Bull, a French company, with a small share of the company held by Samsung. Three companies, very different histories, cultures, skill sets, and experiences, and of course, there were language challenges that impacted understanding and speed. AJ used to call that experience a laboratory of human relationships. It was very rich, and he learned a lot.

A long HRD tenure at 3M followed. The size and